Some Questions and Answers
about God's Covenant
and the Sacrament That Is
a Seal of God's Covenant

Some Questions and Answers about God's Covenant and the Sacrament That Is a Seal of God's Covenant

With Related Texts

By
ROBERT ROLLOCK

Translated and Edited by
AARON CLAY DENLINGER

☙PICKWICK *Publications* · Eugene, Oregon

SOME QUESTIONS AND ANSWERS ABOUT GOD'S COVENANT
AND THE SACRAMENT THAT IS A SEAL OF GOD'S COVENANT
With Related Texts

Copyright © 2016 Aaron Clay Denlinger. All rights reserved. Except for brief quotations in critical publications or reviews, no part of this book may be reproduced in any manner without prior written permission from the publisher. Write: Permissions, Wipf and Stock Publishers, 199 W. 8th Ave., Suite 3, Eugene, OR 97401.

Pickwick Publications
An Imprint of Wipf and Stock Publishers
199 W. 8th Ave., Suite 3
Eugene, OR 97401

www.wipfandstock.com

PAPERBACK ISBN: 978-1-62564-182-3
HARDCOVER ISBN: 978-1-4982-8781-4
EBOOK ISBN: 978-1-4982-9942-8

Cataloguing-in-Publication data:

Names: Rollock, Robert.

Title: Some questions and answers about God's covenant and the sacrament that is a seal of God's covenant : with related texts / Robert Rollock; translated and edited by Aaron Clay Denlinger.

Description: Eugene, OR: Pickwick Publications, 2016 | Includes bibliographical references.

Identifiers: ISBN 978-1-62564-182-3 (paperback) | ISBN 978-1-4982-8781-4 (hardcover) | ISBN 978-1-4982-9942-8 (ebook)

Subjects: LSCH: Rollock, Robert, 1555?–1599. | Reformed Church—Doctrines. | Reformed Church—Scotland—Doctrines—History. | Calvinism—Scotland—History. | Denlinger, Aaron C. (Aaron Clay).

Classification: BX9424.5.S35 R75 2016 (print) | BX9424.5.S35 (ebook)

Manufactured in the U.S.A.   06/10/16

Contents

Acknowledgments | vii

Introduction | 1

Some Questions and Answers about God's Covenant
and the Sacrament That Is the Seal of God's Covenant | 21

On the Covenant of God | 62

On the Sacrament | 65

On Good Works | 78

Bibliography | 95

Acknowledgments

Jesse Atkinson deserves thanks for going above and beyond his duties as my teaching assistant at Reformation Bible College by reviewing the manuscript of this work, noting problems, and making valuable suggestions for improvement. Thanks are also due to the students I've been privileged to teach Latin to over the past twelve years, first at Veritas Christian Academy, then at the University of Aberdeen, and most recently at Reformation Bible College and the Davenant Latin Institute. They have regularly (though perhaps unwittingly) revived my love and enthusiasm for Latin, and so contributed, albeit indirectly, to this present work. I wish to extend particular thanks to an anonymous student at the University of Aberdeen who remarked on his or her evaluation form for LT1509 (Latin II) that "this is by far the funniest class I have ever taken." I consider the comedic value you discovered in my Latin class one of my greatest professional accomplishments. I hope that, in the course of being entertained, you also learned the language. My wife Louise and my children Kaitrin, Geneva, and Austin deserve thanks for the unique way in which they have collectively supported this work—namely, by regularly drawing me away from it and everything else related to my teaching, research, and writing to much more profitable pursuits. *Vobis ago gratias, et vos amo.* At the risk of offending the family members and other worthy persons just noted, I wish to express gratitude to another individual who lives in our home, our German Shepherd Oakley.

Acknowledgments

For the past five years—two of them in Scotland and three of them in Florida—I have walked Oakley every morning, and while doing so have regularly taken advantage of the early morning quiet and relative solitude, not to mention Oakley's apparent lack of interest in conversation, to review aloud Latin declensions and conjugations. Oakley has not once objected to my chanting in a strange language while we walk, though I'm quite certain he would have preferred silence or the odd English phrase he might have understood (for example, "good boy," or "treat"). His indulgence of my strange behavior, and the opportunity it has afforded me to preserve my knowledge of Latin, is much appreciated. So much so, in fact, that I wish to dedicate this book to him, though I'm fairly certain he would rather eat it than read it.

Introduction

"Of our old writers, Rollock, the Scotch divine, is incomparably the best." So judged J. C. Ryle, a nineteenth-century evangelical preacher and author of some repute, in the introduction to his commentary on the gospel of John.[1] Such an opinion of Rollock's worth is not isolated. During his own lifetime Rollock's contemporary Theodore Beza, pastor and scholar in Geneva, claimed that he had "never read or met with anything" among biblical commentaries "more pithily, elegantly, and judiciously written" than Rollock's works on Romans and Ephesians.[2] It is somewhat remarkable, given such testimonies to Rollock's value, that he remains one of the more "neglected figures of Scottish church history."[3]

ROLLOCK'S LIFE AND WORK

Robert Rollock was born in 1555 to minor Scottish nobility near Stirling. Following initial education at the local grammar school, he earned his MA at St. Salvator's College in St. Andrews around 1578, after which he remained at the college teaching philosophy. In 1580 he was appointed examiner for the faculty of arts at St. Leonard's College, and around the same time began studying

---

1. Quoted in Woolsey, "Rollock," 3.
2. Rollock, *Works*, 1:10.
3. Woolsey, "Rollock," 2.

biblical Hebrew under James Melville at St. Mary's. In 1583 he was invited to assume the reins of a new college in Edinburgh (today the University of Edinburgh). Particularly instrumental in bringing Rollock to Edinburgh were James Lawson, the minister of St. Giles who had formerly taught Hebrew in St. Andrews and served as sub-principal of King's College in Aberdeen, and William Little, a baillie who would shortly be elected provost in Scotland's capital. Rollock delivered his inaugural address—"a brilliant address which gained him universal admiration" according to one contemporary—to the new university on October 1st of that year.[4]

Rollock spent the next several years leading the college's first class through the entirety of the new institution's liberal arts curriculum. During those same years he contributed much to his students' theological formation—and served as a conduit of continental Reformed thought to Scotland—by lecturing on Beza's *Quaestiones et responsiones* and the Heidelberg Catechism on Saturday and Sunday afternoons respectively.[5] From 1587 onward he devoted himself more fully to the roles of principal and professor of theology in the college, and to regular preaching in one of Edinburgh's parish kirks.[6] The year 1590 witnessed Rollock's first publication, a commentary—based on his university lectures—on Paul's Epistle to the Ephesians. During the decade of life remaining to Rollock, published commentaries on Daniel (1591), Romans (1593), First and Second Thessalonians and Philemon (1598), select Psalms (1599), and the gospel of John (1599) followed. His curriculum vitae eventually included three posthumously published commentaries—Colossians (1600), Galatians (1602), and Hebrews (1605)—as well as a manuscript commentary on 1 Peter. Nearly all Rollock's published commentaries saw multiple editions on the continent, testimony to the man's reputation and influence beyond the borders of his native Scotland.[7] Rollock's labors as

---

4. Rollock, *Works*, 1:xxxix–lxv.

5. Ibid., 1:lxv–lxvi.

6. Woolsey, "Rollock," 7–9.

7. A bibliography of Rollock's works can be found in Rollock, *Works*, 1:xc–xcv.

Introduction

principal, preacher, writer, and teacher were cut short by a fairly premature death—he had just turned forty-four—in February of 1599. He left behind him a wife Helen, who was pregnant with their first child (a daughter, Jean) when he died.[8]

ROLLOCK'S ROLE IN THE DEVELOPMENT OF REFORMED COVENANT THEOLOGY

Despite Rollock's accomplishments and reputation in his own day as a biblical commentator (reflected both in Beza's praise for his work, noted above, and in the multiple editions of his commentaries), Rollock is best remembered today for the role he purportedly played in the development of covenant theology (a.k.a. "federal theology" or "federalism") in the Reformed tradition.[9] Indeed, it is difficult to find scholarly treatments of Rollock today that approach him from any other angle.[10] The present work is no exception, though it does hope to offer something new—both in the translations that constitute the body of this work and here in the introduction to the same—to scholarly perspectives on Rollock's significance as a covenant theologian.

To date, scholarly analysis of Rollock's covenant thought and the role he played in the development of Reformed covenant theology has been almost entirely based on Rollock's discussion of God's covenants with man in the first several chapters of his

---

8. Rollock, *Works*, 1:lxxx–lxxxvii.

9. Michael McGiffert names Rollock "the first full-fledged federalist" on the basis of Rollock's mature treatment of the covenant of works in addition to the covenant of grace in the Scottish divine's 1597 *Tractatus de vocatione efficaci* ("Perkinsian Moment," 146). Works which explore Rollock's role in the development of Reformed covenant theology in some detail include Denlinger, "Rollock on Covenant and Sacrament"; Denlinger, "Rollock's Catechism"; Fesko, *Westminster Assembly*, 135–36; Isbell, "Covenant of Works," 41–51; Letham, "*Foedus Operum*," 457–67; Macedo, "Covenant Theology of Rollock"; Woolsey, *Unity and Continuity*, 512–39.

10. There are notable exceptions, including Backus, "Piscator Misconstrued"; Ellis, "Eternal Decree"; Garner, "Discourse Analysis."

1597 *Tractatus de vocatione efficaci*.¹¹ Very little attention—indeed, none at all by most scholars—has been given to Rollock's 1596 *Quaestiones et responsiones aliquot de Foedere Dei: deque Sacramento quod Foederis Dei sigillum est*, or to relevant passages in his biblical commentaries that explore the subject of God's covenants with man. This is partially due to the substantial overlap between the content of Rollock's 1596 catechism and those chapters of the 1597 work on effectual calling that treat the covenants. In other words, Andrew Woolsey, who does make mention of Rollock's catechism, is largely correct to observe with reference to the same that "the substance of this rare work was incorporated into a larger treatise on effectual calling, and published the following year as *Tractatus de vocatione efficaci* (1597)."¹² Neglect of Rollock's catechism and commentaries in discussions of his covenant thought stems more substantially, however, from the relative inaccessibility of those works in comparison to the 1597 work on effectual calling. Shortly after Rollock's death, a London preacher named Henry Holland produced an English translation of the 1597 *Tractatus* titled *A Treatise of God's Effectual Calling* (1603). That work was incorporated into a two-volume edition of Rollock's works (in English translation) by the Wodrow Society in the nineteenth century, which edition was reprinted in 2008 by Reformation Heritage Books. Neither Rollock's catechism nor his biblical commentaries, by way of contrast, have been translated or reproduced in modern editions/reprints.¹³

Exclusive attention to Rollock's 1597 *Tractatus* in judgments about his role in the development of Reformed covenant thought is attended by certain problems. For one thing, there are

---

11. See Rollock, *Works*, 1:33–55.

12. Woolsey, *Unity and Continuity*, 512.

13. The present volume incorporates two of my own previous efforts at translating Rollock. In 2009 I published a translation of the first half of Rollock's catechism (Denlinger, "Rollock's Catechism") in *Mid-America Journal of Theology*. In 2013 I published translations of two short sections of Rollock's Romans commentary (Denlinger, "Rollock on Covenant and Sacrament") in *Reformation & Renaissance Review*. The translations comprised in those articles are reproduced here with permission, albeit with slight revision.

Introduction

aspects of Rollock's thinking on the divine covenants that surface much more clearly in his catechism and commentaries than in his treatise on effectual calling. So, for example, the way in which Rollock's ideas about God's covenants (both before and after the fall) inform his thinking on the sacraments (both before and after the fall) becomes apparent from the catechism, which takes both covenant and sacrament as its themes, but not from the 1597 *Tractatus*, which contains scarcely a word on the sacraments. More substantial problems, perhaps, attend the oversight of Rollock's catechism and commentaries in efforts to parse how and when discrete covenantal concepts appeared in Reformed writings of the late sixteenth-century, or in closely related (if arguably unfruitful) efforts to determine who influenced whom in the progress of covenantal ideas.

An example of the latter problem presents itself in the tendency to situate Rollock to the right of certain English divines—especially Dudley Fenner and William Perkins—in chronological surveys of early modern Reformed treatments of a pre-fall covenant, and/or to assume that Rollock was directly indebted to those English divines in his own thinking about such a covenant.[14] Thus Woolsey: "Rollock's teaching on the legal and evangelical covenants clearly followed the pattern of Perkins."[15] Such a move supports the more general conclusion that "the covenantal thought of ... early Scottish theologians stands in the mainstream of Reformed theological tradition, its headwaters originating in Geneva and flowing through Heidelberg and Elizabethan Puritanism."[16] The supposition of some "influence of ... English Puritan sources" on Rollock's covenant thought in particular rests on the observation that Fenner and Perkins published writings contrasting the covenants of works and grace in 1585 (Fenner's *Sacra theologia*) and 1590 (Perkins's *Armilla aurea*) respectively, six years before

---

14. See, for example, Isbell, "Covenant of Works," 35–50; Woolsey, *Unity and Continuity*, 442–539.

15. Woolsey, *Unity and Continuity*, 516. See also pp. 535–39, which offer more detailed analysis of Rollock's influences.

16. Ibid., 535.

Rollock published his catechism on God's covenants and subsequent *Tractatus*. Rollock's familiarity with Perkins' writings by 1596 is taken for granted, perhaps rightly. His familiarity with Fenner's work cannot so easily be assumed; Woolsey does, however, note that one of Rollock's own printers, Robert Waldegrave, published two of Fenner's works (though not the *Sacra theologia*) in Edinburgh in 1592, thereby rendering Rollock's familiarity with Fenner by the time he began carving out his own covenantal ideas likely.[17]

Yet closer scrutiny of Perkin's work and a quick glance at Rollock's commentaries soon problematizes this narrative. There is, first of all, the fact that Perkins actually makes no mention of a pre-fall covenant or *foedus operum* ("covenant of works") in the 1590 *Armilla aurea*. In 1591 Perkins published a second—and very much expanded—edition of the *Armilla*, which edition served as the basis for an English translation completed the same year.[18] In that (and later) editions Perkins named "God's covenant [*foedus*] and the seal of that covenant" as the "external means" by which God executes his eternal decree of election. He went on to define "God's covenant" as "his pact [*pactum*] with man concerning the obtaining of eternal life under certain conditions," and to name God's covenant as *duplex*, comprising "the covenant of works [*foedus operum*] and the covenant of grace." He further defined *foedus operum* as "the covenant of God that includes a condition of perfect obedience and is expressed in the moral law." And finally, he named the Decalogue as "the epitome of the whole law and the covenant of works."[19] In 1590, by way of contrast, Perkins

---

17. Ibid., 516.

18. While the 1590 *Armilla* ran to roughly 66 pages, the 1591 *Armilla* ran to well over 300 (of identical size and similar font).

19. Perkins, *Armilla* (1591), F2r–F2v. Perkins, it should be noted, does not identify this covenant of works as a pre-fall arrangement. References to Jer 32:31 and Gal 4:24 in his discussion of the *foedus operum* suggest he primarily envisioned the "covenant of works" as a principle of inheritance on the basis of perfect obedience established *after* the fall, a principle embodied especially in the Decalogue, a principle which served to prompt sinners to despair of their self-righteousness and take refuge in God's gratuitous promise of life on the

identified "the preaching of the Word and the administration of the sacraments" as the "external means" by which God executes his decree of election. He named the Word as *duplex*, comprising "both law and gospel," and proceeded to an examination of the Decalogue as the "epitome of the whole law" without a single reference to God's covenant(s).[20]

Such nitpicking about the precise date of Perkins' first reference to "the legal and evangelical covenants" assumes some significance, perhaps, when juxtaposed with Rollock's comments on God's covenants in his 1590 Ephesians commentary, a work based on his lectures from the late 1580s. Commenting on Eph 1:7, Rollock noted that every spiritual benefit ultimately enjoyed by believers is founded upon God's decree. He identified God's promise in time as God's means of executing his eternal decree, and then added:

> But the promise should be referred to the covenant. Therefore, something should be said briefly about the covenant, which we acknowledge as the source of this benefit of our redemption. God, then, has established a twofold covenant [*foedus duplex*] with man from the beginning: one natural, established in creation itself, containing the law; the other a covenant of grace, established with man after the fall, containing the gospel.[21]

As demonstrated below, Rollock expanded upon this doctrine of divine covenants considerably in his 1593 Romans commentary. But even this terse comment about God's twofold covenant in 1590 raises questions about the supposed English Puritan, or at least Perkinsian, influence upon Rollock. There is, to be sure, affinity between Rollock's comments here and Perkins' comments in the 1591 *Armilla*, not only in the recognition of God's covenant as *duplex*, but in the recognition (and statement of such in the immediate context) of God's covenant as the means by which God executes his decree of election. But, needless to say, the earlier

---

basis of Christ's obedience and sacrifice.
20. Perkins, *Armilla* (1590), 15v.
21. Rollock, *Epistolam ad Ephesios*, 18.

date of Rollock's comments in this regard precludes the possibility of his indebtedness to Perkins on these matters. Indeed, the earlier date of Rollock's comments establish the possibility (however slight) that influence moved in the opposite direction (that is, from Scotland to England), particularly so in light of Perkins' decision to replace "proclamation of the Word" with God's *duplex* covenant as the means by which God executes his saving decree in the 1591 edition of his work.[22]

Of course, Rollock's reflections upon God's *foedus duplex* from 1590 do not prohibit the possibility of Fenner's influence on him. Indeed, they might even strengthen the case for Fenner's influence since Rollock's earliest apparent reference to God's twofold covenant bears a noticeable degree of affinity to Fenner's reference to the same in his *Sacra theologia* (1585). Fenner introduced the subject of "God's covenant" in the fourth book of his *Sacra theologia*, immediately on the heels of a discussion of sin. Having defined *Foedus Dei* as "the covenant concerning life and death, established with man and his descendants," and having noted that God's covenant involves two voluntary actions (God's *stipulatio* and man's reception of the same), he observed that "God's covenant is *duplex*," comprising "the covenant of works" and "the covenant of gratuitous promise." He then defined "the covenant of works" as "that covenant in which the annexed condition is perfect obedience," and outlined a *duplex* function for that covenant "in the realization of predestination." The covenant of works, he explained, served to "shut the mouth of the whole world and render it liable to God's condemnation (Rom 3.19)," and to "make apparent man's sin and

---

22. Attention to Rollock's earliest account of God's *duplex* covenant with man likewise problematizes the assumption that Robert Howie, a Scottish student of Caspar Olevian's in Herborn in the later 1580s, constituted an "important link" (Woolsey, *Unity and Continuity*, 517) between Rollock and the Heidelberg (covenant) theologians, an assumption that rests at least in part on Howie's 1591 publication *De reconciliatione hominis cum Deo*. In that work Howie contrasted God's gratuitous covenant, serving as the instrument of sinful man's reconciliation to God, with "that covenant which God established with Adam in creation (which covenant was afterwards published in the law), according to which Adam was obligated to render perfect obedience to God in his own strength" (Howie, *De reconciliatione*, 15).

Introduction

misery" in order that elect sinners "might be impelled to seek restoration in the gratuitous covenant." Whether Rollock was familiar with Fenner's *Sacra theologia*, published in London in 1585 and again in Geneva in 1586 and 1589, is difficult to establish with any degree of certainty. Regardless, it should be noted that Rollock's earliest reference to a "natural" covenant—a covenant that he rebranded *foedus operum* in 1593, using terminology by then employed by both Fenner and Perkins—explicitly situates that covenant before the fall ("established in creation itself"), a unique feature of Rollock's doctrine vis-a-vis both Fenner's and Perkins's teachings, and one that received considerable elaboration in his Romans commentary and 1596 catechism.[23]

In any case, widening our scope to include Rollock's more detailed considerations of God's covenant of works with man from 1593 onward immediately brings into focus aspects of his teaching that increasingly distinguish it from both English Puritan and continental predecessors. Of course, "nothing comes from nothing," a principle argued by Parmenides and popularized by Maria that applies to histories of doctrine as well as anything else. But Rollock does genuinely seem to have been an innovative thinker when it came to the particular subject of God's covenant with man prior to the fall.

ROLLOCK'S COVENANT THEOLOGY RECONSIDERED IN LIGHT OF THE PRESENT TRANSLATION

In turning to consider the texts translated in whole (the catechism) or in part (the Romans commentary) in this book, I should note that, despite the preceding comments, it is not ultimately my intention to advance any particular argument (or counter-argument) regarding influences on Rollock's covenant thought, and/

---

23. The particular functions that Fenner ascribes to the covenant of works suggest that, like Perkins, he envisioned the same primarily as a post-fall principle of inheritance on the basis of works, a principle embodied especially in the moral law.

or to champion any detailed grand narrative regarding the development of covenant theology within post-Reformation Reformed theology. I do intend, rather more simply and mundanely, to highlight unique aspects of Rollock's teaching on the covenants, or more precisely, unique aspects of his teaching on the pre-fall covenant, that become apparent from the broader survey of Rollock's writings on the covenant that the translations offered here allow. The particular aspects of Rollock's teaching I have in mind will, I suspect, be recognized by students of seventeenth-century Reformed thought as fairly standard features of the more developed Reformed covenant theologies of that (and later) period(s). Such, I think, reflects Rollock's influence on subsequent Reformed covenant theologians, both in Scotland and abroad. To all appearances, Rollock left his stamp upon a certain trajectory within Reformed theology that made increasing use in subsequent years of the covenant motif to structure accounts of specific doctrines such as Scripture, anthropology, or soteriology, as well as surveys of salvation history *in toto* and/or accounts of Reformed doctrine as a systematic whole.

Ideally a claim regarding unique features in Rollock's doctrine of the pre-fall covenant would proceed from a thorough survey of earlier treatments of that supposed entity by Reformed thinkers. Such a survey would include consideration of published comments on the pre-fall covenant/*foedus operum* by Zacharias Ursinus, Caspar Olevianus, Johannes Piscator, Fenner and Perkins (whose comments are sufficiently noted above), Robert Howie, and Amandus Polanus in the years leading up to Rollock's 1596 catechism, as well perhaps as unpublished (as of 1596) comments on the subject by Thomas Cartwright and Franciscus Junius. Such a survey cannot realistically be included here.[24] Suffice it to say that Reformed comments on a pre-fall covenant or *foedus operum* prior to 1596 are generally as abbreviated, or even more so, than those by Fenner and Perkins reviewed above, and rarely if ever move beyond those by Fenner and Perkins in detailing any theological significance to such a covenant. In my judgment, Amandus

24. Most helpful for those interested in such is Isbell's "Covenant of Works."

Introduction

Polanus's comments on the *foedus operum* in his 1590 *Partitiones theologicae* represent the fullest treatment of that subject prior to Rollock's, but even those comments barely fill a single page of text. Polanus, much in the vein of Fenner, named God's "eternal covenant"—that is, the "covenant in which God promises man eternal life"—as *duplex*, embracing both "the covenant of works and the covenant of grace." He defined the *foedus operum* as "God's pact [*pactum*] made with man concerning eternal life, to which is joined both a condition of perfect obedience to be fulfilled by man and a threat of eternal death should he not render perfect obedience." Significantly, Polanus's citation of Gen 2:17 to support this definition of the *foedus operum* and subsequent note that "repetition of the covenant of works was made by God" at Sinai mark that *explicit* situating of the *foedus operum* before the fall that is lacking in Fenner and Perkins. Polanus, finally, identified four functions to the covenant of works (as such is encountered in the moral law): it serves, first of all, to excite men to obedience; secondly, to render all men liable to God's punishment on account of their failures in obedience; thirdly, to expose sin and wickedness; and fourthly, to impel men to seek restoration in the covenant of grace.[25]

The abbreviated nature of comments on the pre-fall covenant prior to the publication of Rollock's catechism in 1596 points to the first and rather obvious unique aspect of Rollock's teaching—namely, that he treats the pre-fall covenant at much greater length than earlier writers. Indeed, Rollock constitutes the first Reformed writer to treat the covenant of works beneath its own discrete heading. His catechism is divided into three overarching sections, the first titled "Concerning, first of all, God's covenant in general, and then the covenant of works," the second titled "Concerning the Covenant of Grace," and the third titled "Concerning the Sacrament in General." The apparently unprecedented decision to give the covenant of works its own discrete heading lends itself,

---

25. Polanus, *Partitiones theologicae*, 79–80. Although Polanus expands slightly upon Fenner's comments on the *foedus operum*, the similarities in structure and language between their comments strongly suggest Polanus's familiarity with and dependence on Fenner.

of course, to a more robust discussion of that entity. Of the 102 questions and answers that Rollock ultimately devotes to the covenants, 28 (qs. 3–30) are specifically dedicated to the covenant of works, a continuous section spanning roughly eight pages of text. Yet such figures only partially reflect the extent of Rollock's engagement with the covenant of works in his text, since that subject figures into substantial sections of his discussion of the covenant of grace (see qs. 31, 37–38, 41–42, 57, 64, 72–73, 76, and 89–90) and his discussion of the sacraments (see qs. 102–105). While Rollock's lengthier treatment of the covenant of works vis-a-vis earlier Reformed writers may not seem particularly important, it is an obvious step towards a theology that attributes structural significance and ascribes substantial dogmatic functions to the notion of a pre-fall covenant between God and man.

Secondly (and more substantively), Rollock's teaching is unique in the pronounced role that it attributes to the covenant of works as both a theological and redemptive-historical foil to the covenant of grace. Earlier writers anticipated Rollock in this regard. Their terse descriptions of the *foedus operum* as a covenant promising eternal life upon condition of perfect obedience were clearly intended to form a point of contrast and comparison for the covenant of grace, in which eternal life is freely offered to sinners. But Rollock discovers much greater potential in the covenant of works to highlight features of the covenant of grace and that salvation offered to sinners therein. His attention to the pre-fall covenant's foundation (q. 6), promise (q. 7), condition (q. 8), historical location (q. 15), manner of establishment (q. 16), repetition in redemptive history (q. 18), manner of repetition in redemptive history (q. 19), function in redemptive history (q. 21), initial violation (q. 25), subsequent violation (q. 27), penalty (q. 28), and location in the biblical canon (q. 30) all serve, ultimately, to emphasize contrasting features of the covenant of grace. To note one example of how he develops such contrasts: Rollock identifies in q. 62 the condition of the covenant of grace as "faith in the mediator," notes that faith is a product of grace rather than man's innate powers (q. 63), and then observes, alluding to his earlier consideration of the pre-fall covenant's condition (q. 8), that faith as the gracious covenant's condition necessarily excludes "those good works of nature that were named as the condition of the covenant of works," since "Christ and God's mercy, which are the objects of faith, cannot—in the justification of man—consist with the powers of man's nature or the works that proceed from that nature" (q. 64). At the risk of stating the rather obvious, this particular contrast between the covenant of works and covenant of grace ultimately serves to reinforce Protestant teaching on the exclusive and instrumental role that faith plays in justification.

Thirdly, Rollock's teaching is unique in the way that it employs the covenant of works to frame an account and analysis of Christ's obedience (as itself an aspect of Christ's work). Rollock, in other words, is the first Reformed theologian to my knowledge to refer to Christ as one "born under the covenant of works" and "liable to the same" (q. 37), or as one who has "fulfilled the covenant of works," (q. 38) both "by doing [*agendo*] and by suffering [*patiendo*]" (q. 39). These claims, for Rollock, lead on to a substantial discussion about Christ's life of obedience and his passion, and how both contribute to man's ultimate salvation (qs. 40–49). At one level, of course, the move to frame an account of Christ's work by reference to the covenant of works is obvious and inevitable once man's pre-fall experience has come to be defined with reference to that covenant. Christ, after all, is named in Scripture as the second (or last) Adam (cf. 1 Cor 15:45 & Rom 5:15), and as one "born under the law" (Gal 4:4), which "law" Reformed theologians recognized as promulgated upon tables of stone at Sinai but equally, and previously, written upon man's heart in creation.[26] Nevertheless, the concrete move to place the second Adam "under the covenant of works" and to frame an account of his work with reference to the same (over and above the law) was not without

26. Isbell's comment ("Covenant of Works," 21) regarding Ursinus could arguably be extended to each Reformed writer who preceded Rollock in referencing a pre-fall covenant/*foedus operum*: "Ursinus *by implication* conceives of Christ as fulfilling the terms of the creation covenant" (emphasis mine). Rollock makes explicit that which was arguably implicit in earlier Reformed writers.

theological consequence. An understanding of Christ as one born under and fulfilling that covenant which God established with man before the fall found expression in, and had bearing upon, a number of intramural Reformed debates of the seventeenth century, such as that on the imputation of Christ's active obedience to believers, or that on what man's eschatological future would have been—heavenly, glorified life or perpetual, earthly existence—had Adam remained upright. It also found expression in, and had bearing upon, discussions about the meritorious nature of Adam's hypothetical obedience in the covenant of works. Rollock, interestingly, denies in his catechism that Adam's good works would have had the proper essence of merit in the *foedus operum* (qs. 12–13). In the seventeenth-century an increasing number of Reformed theologians demurred on this point and, with an eye towards the meritorious nature of that obedience rendered by the second Adam under the covenant of works, argued that the first Adam's obedience would likewise have been meritorious, even if "merit" was ultimately defined by such thinkers not with reference to any intrinsic value of said hypothetical works but to God's free determination of an appropriate reward for the same.[27]

A fourth and final unique aspect of Rollock's teaching on the pre-fall covenant does not present itself in the translations offered below, but nevertheless warrants mention here in order to round out our consideration of Rollock's significance to the development of Reformed covenant theology. This final, unique aspect of Rollock's teaching presents itself in the chapter on original sin in Rollock's 1597 *Tractatus*, in which chapter Rollock suggests—a first among Reformed thinkers, at least to my knowledge—that the pre-fall covenant *per se* functioned as the actual basis for humankind's solidarity with Adam, and thus for humankind's voluntariety of, and culpability for, Adam's actual transgression in the Garden. Having asked "from whence" that transgression—that is, Adam's eating of the forbidden fruit in the Garden of Eden—derived its "power [*efficacia*] to be propagated to each and every descendant of Adam," Rollock contends that such "power" sprung not from

---

27. See, for example, Braun, *Doctrina foederum*, 259–60.

Introduction

the reality of any natural or intrinsic relationship between Adam and his descendants, but from "a certain covenant of God which he established with Adam in the first creation."[28] To state the matter otherwise, Rollock understands humankind's culpability for Adam's transgression to rest ultimately on God's institution of solidarity between Adam and his descendants, which institution found expression from the very first in God's explicit statement that "if man should stand firm in that innocence in which he was created, he would stand firm for himself and his descendants, but if on the contrary he should not stand firm and should rather fall, he would fall for himself and for his descendants."[29]

Previous Reformed theologians had, of course, accepted humankind's solidarity with Adam and culpability for Adam's transgression, but they had been content to let humankind's physical descent from Adam and universal participation in human nature jointly serve as the theoretical basis for that solidarity and culpability. Even those who had identified the law written on Adam's heart—or, like Augustine, the law prohibiting consumption of the forbidden fruit—as a covenant, and thus either explicitly or implicitly named Adam's offspring *in toto* as covenant-breakers, had so implicated Adam's descendants by virtue of an acknowledged solidarity with Adam ultimately premised upon the concept of human nature.[30] Subsequent Reformed theologians, on the other hand, would increasingly follow Rollock's lead, acknowledging both a federal relationship—that is, a relationship premised upon the pre-fall *foedus*—between Adam and his posterity serving as the basis for humankind's culpability for Adam's sin, and a real/natural relationship between the same serving as the basis for

---

28. Rollock, *Tractatus*, 193–94.

29. Ibid., 194.

30. For Augustine's comments on the pre-fall covenant and its violation by Adam and his descendants, see "On Marriage and Concupiscence," 292. For a fuller explanation of Augustine's perspective on the basis of humankind's solidarity with Adam, and some comparison of the same to the doctrines of Anselm, Thomas Aquinas, and Calvin, see Denlinger, "Calvin's Understanding," 226–50.

humankind's inheritance of corruption and perversity.³¹ Thus, for instance, Anthony Burgess in his book on original sin: "by God's covenant we were looked upon as in [Adam]."³²

While Rollock apparently constitutes the earliest *Reformed* thinker to explicitly premise humankind's solidarity with Adam and culpability for Adam's sin upon a covenant between God and Adam in the garden, he was not the first theologian *per se* to do so in his century. In a series of publications between 1532 and 1551, and during proceedings of the Council of Trent in 1546, an Italian Dominican friar named Ambrogio Catarino had challenged the adequacy of the concept of universal human nature to explain universal solidarity with Adam and culpability for Adam's sin, and had promoted the idea that God established a covenant with Adam in the Garden that served as the basis for said solidarity and culpability. Catarino's doctrine of a pre-fall covenant—a covenant specifically serving to establish humankind's voluntariety of, and culpability for, Adam's sin—was forcefully rejected by his Dominican contemporary Domingo de Soto (among others), but was embraced, at least in some form, by a number of contemporary and immediately subsequent Roman Catholic thinkers, including Juan Morillo (who, interestingly, converted to the Reformed faith in the early 1550s), Alfonso Salmeron, Gabriel Vasquez, Francisco Suarez, and Adam Tanner.³³ Rollock was very likely familiar with Catarino's teaching on the covenant (and perhaps to some extent with the minor controversy Catarino's doctrine caused in Roman Catholic circles)—he engaged Catarino's overall teaching on original sin in the course of his own chapter on the subject in the *Tractatus*.³⁴ To all appearances, then, Rollock's own insistence that God's covenant with Adam in the Garden constitutes the proper

---

31. See, for example, Turretin, *Institutes*, 1:616.

32. Burgess, *Original sin*, 46.

33. I have explored this subject in considerable detail in Denlinger, *Omnes in Adam*.

34. Rollock, *Tractatus*, 195–96. Rollock does not, admittedly, make explicit reference to Catarino's idea of a pre-fall covenant. Nevertheless, his reference to Catarino's doctrine suggests familiarity with one or more of Catarino's works on original sin, all of which comprise extended discussion of the covenant.

Introduction

basis for humankind's solidarity with Adam and culpability for Adam's sin marks a concrete—albeit unacknowledged, for obvious reasons—debt to Catarino.[35]

Further unique aspects of Rollock's treatment of the pre-fall covenant vis-a-vis earlier Reformed treatments of that doctrine could, I suspect, be noted. The four unique aspects of his doctrine just identified, however, should serve to establish Rollock's place as a pivotal figure in the development of Reformed covenant theology, particularly so since the aspects in question increasingly became, as intimated previously, standard features of seventeenth-century Reformed teaching on the divine covenants.

NOTES ON TEXT AND TRANSLATION

The main body of this work comprises a complete translation of Rollock's 1596 *Quaestiones et responsiones aliquot de Foedere Dei: deque Sacramento quod Foederis Dei sigillum est*. In 2009 I published a translation of the first half of Rollock's catechism—that half dealing directly with the covenants—in *Mid-America Journal of Theology*.[36] In revisiting Rollock's catechism sometime later, I realized that a translation of the entire catechism would be useful for at least three reasons: first of all, because it's preferable to have any work translated in its entirety rather than in part, especially so for students of that work's author or doctrinal themes; secondly, because the latter half of Rollock's catechism—that half dealing with the sacraments—provides further illustration of the theological utility that Rollock discovered in God's *duplex foedus*, and so stands to enrich our appreciation for Rollock's covenant thought; and thirdly, because Rollock's existing works in translation include nothing on the subject of the sacraments, and access to his thoughts

---

35. See my more extended comments on Rollock's doctrine in relation to Catarino's in Denlinger, *Omnes in Adam*, 265–70.

36. Denlinger, "Rollock's Catechism." As noted previously, my earlier work appears here with permission. I should note that I have revisited my translation of the first half of Rollock's catechism for this publication and have, I hope, made some improvements.

on that subject might serve both students of Rollock's theology and students of early modern (Scottish) Reformed Sacramentology. Rollock's questions and answers on the sacraments—appearing here for the first time in translation—stand, in other words, to buttress the claims I have made above about Rollock's significance as a covenant theologian, and to inform scholarly judgments about various claims that have been made concerning post-Reformation Scottish thought on baptism and the Lord's Supper.[37]

Rollock dedicated his catechism to William Little, the public official who had been instrumental in bringing him to Edinburgh. Rollock's letter of dedication marks his recognition of Little's patronage and paternal care for him. Little apparently had a son, also named William, enrolled at the University of Edinburgh when Rollock published his work. Rollock makes mention of the younger Little in his dedication, observing with good, humanist humility that his "small trifle" of a catechism comprises questions "about God's covenant and the sacraments that are childish [*pueriles*]" but might "be useful to children [*pueres*] and students of the rudiments," not least William Little's son. Rollock actually sounds a rather ambivalent note regarding the younger William Little, expressing his hope that the son might eventually achieve the virtues of his father, but suggesting that if he does not, the failure "must be imputed to the son himself and not to the father." One gets the impression Rollock would like to have added, perhaps on behalf of the entire university, "or to us."[38]

My translation of Rollock's catechism itself is, I think, fairly straightforward. The headings included throughout the catechism are original to his work. The only real liberty I have taken in

---

37. I think specifically of M. Charles Bell's claim that a Scottish Reformed emphasis upon the covenantal nature of God's relationship with his people resulted in movement away from a properly Calvinistic Eucharistic theology towards a notion of the Lord's Supper as "little more than a badge of repentance and election." Bell, *Calvin and Scottish Theology*, 9. Though Rollock, by virtue of the texts translated in this volume, can speak for himself, it's my impression that his (covenantal) treatment of the sacraments significantly undermines Bell's claim.

38. Rollock, *Questiones et responsiones*, A2r–A2v.

translation is the addition of consecutive numbers to the questions. I added these on the assumption that they might prove a useful tool for persons wishing to reference Rollock's catechism in the future. I have kept critical commentary to a minimum, very occasionally noting Rollock's mistaken referencing of biblical proof-texts, highlighting the significance that a particular point made might have to scholarly questions/debates about early modern covenant theology, and/or pointing readers towards earlier questions that illumine the meaning of later ones that, at least in my judgment, seem slightly difficult to understand on their own.

Also included in this volume are three translated sections from Robert Rollock's 1593 Romans commentary. The three sections in question were titled by Rollock himself "On the Covenant of God," "On the Sacrament," and "On Good Works." These particular sections of his work on Romans appeared in a series of short, doctrinal summaries that Rollock inserted between commentary on Romans 8:30 and Romans 8:31 in order to explicate in greater detail those divine benefits concisely comprehended in Scripture's reference (in Rom 8:29–30) to the foreknowledge, predestination, calling, justification, and glorification of believers.[39]

My decision to translate these specific theological tracts reflects recognition of the significant use they make, each in its own particular way, of the notion of a pre-fall covenant. The content of the first two tracts—"On the Covenant of God" and "On the Sacrament"—very much corresponds with the content of Rollock's catechism in its respective halves. "On Good Works" covers unique ground in relation to the subject of Rollock's catechism, and thereby discloses unique theological potential for the *foedus operum*. Though covering much ground in common with Rollock's catechism, these selections from Rollock's Romans commentary belong to a different genre of literature, and thus it is my hope that they might serve to illumine his doctrine as discovered in the catechism (and vice versa). These texts have added historical interest insofar as they belonged to a publication that was substantially

---

39. See J. V. Fesko's comments on this section of Rollock's Romans commentary in *Beyond Calvin*, 86.

more popular and influential in Rollock's day than either his 1596 catechism or his 1597 *Tractatus*, at least if popularity and influence be measured by publication history. Rollock's Romans commentary saw two editions in Edinburgh (1593 and 1594) and three editions in Geneva (1595, 1596, and 1608). It seems very likely that it served as the *primary* vehicle for the transmission of Rollock's covenantal ideas to others.

An earlier effort of mine to translate Rollock's "On the Covenant of God" and "On the Sacrament" appeared in 2013 in *Reformation & Renaissance Review* under the title "Robert Rollock on covenant and sacrament: two texts." That earlier work appears here with permission, but it should be noted that—as with the section of Rollock's catechism previously published but appearing here—I have revisited, revised, and I hope improved my earlier work for this volume. My resulting and final translation of these texts is, like that of the catechism, fairly straightforward in my judgment. I have taken the necessary liberties with punctuation and word order that translation from Latin to English requires, but none I hope with Rollock's meaning. Perhaps one item worth noting is that I have followed the paragraph divisions found in the Geneva publications of Rollock's Romans commentary, even though these were almost certainly introduced by the Genevan printer rather than Rollock. In the original Edinburgh edition of the work, Rollock (or his printer) proved far too reluctant on the matter of paragraph breaks for modern tastes.

Some Questions and Answers about God's Covenant and the Sacrament That Is the Seal of God's Covenant

CONCERNING, FIRST OF ALL, GOD'S COVENANT IN GENERAL, AND THEN THE COVENANT OF WORKS

1. **Question**: *What is the covenant of God established with man?*[1]

   Answer: It is that by which God promises man something good under some settled condition, and man accepts the condition.

2. **Q:** *How manifold is the covenant of God established with man?*

   A: It is twofold: there is the covenant of nature or works, and the covenant of grace. Gal 4:24.

3. **Q:** *What is the covenant of nature or works?*

   A: It is the covenant of God in which he promises man eternal life under the condition of good works proceeding

---

1. Literally "the covenant of God *struck* with man." The Latin phrase *percutere foedus* mirrors ancient Hebrew idiom. See Muller, "Covenant of Works," 83.

from the powers of man's nature, and man accepts that condition of good works. Lev 18:5; Rom 10:5; Gal 3:12.

4. **Q:** *Was there no grave threat added to the promise of this covenant?*
   A: One was added.

5. **Q:** *In what form?*
   A: "Cursed is anyone who does not continue in all the things which are written in the Book of the Law, in order to do them." Gen 2:17; Deut 27:26; Gal 3:10.[2]

6. **Q:** *What is the foundation of the covenant of works?*
   A: A good, holy, and upright nature—the kind of nature that existed in man by creation. For if God had not made man after his own image—that is, wise, holy, and righteous by nature—he surely could not have established with him this covenant, which has for its condition holy, just, and perfect works of nature. Gen 1:26-27; Eph 4:24; Col 3:9.

7. **Q:** *What is promised in the covenant of works?*
   A: A blessed life enduring forever. Rom 10:5; Gal 3:12.

8. **Q:** *What is the condition in the covenant of works?*

---

2. Elsewhere Rollock identifies this same "threat" as the major premise of a syllogism which in its entirety constitutes the "doctrine of the Law." He writes: "The whole doctrine of the Law may be reduced to this syllogism: Cursed is he that continueth not in all things which are written in the book of this law, to do them; but I have not continued in them; therefore I am accursed." This stands in contrast to "the doctrine of the Gospel [which] may be comprehended in this [syllogistic] form: Whosoever believeth shall be justified and live; But I believe; therefore I shall be justified and live" (Rollock, *Works*, 1:194–95). The correlation of "covenant of works" with "Law" and "covenant of grace" with "Gospel"—evident here and throughout Rollock's catechism—supports Michael Horton's argument that early Reformed theology's twofold covenant scheme largely served to maintain the law/gospel distinction which was central to both Lutheran and Reformed expressions of the Protestant faith. See Horton, "Law, Gospel, and Covenant," 279–87.

The Covenant and the Sacrament

A: The condition is good works, which should proceed from that good, holy, and upright nature upon which the covenant itself was founded. Rom 10:5; Gal 3:12.

9. **Q:** *What realities are excluded by this condition?*

    A: By this condition, first, faith in Christ, and second, works proceeding from grace and regeneration are excluded from the covenant of works. Rom 11:6.

10. **Q:** *Why are these realities excluded?*

    A: Because the virtues of man's nature, along with its works, cannot consist together with the grace of Christ and works of grace. Rom 11:6.

11. **Q:** *What are the heads of this covenant's condition?*

    A: They are comprised one apiece in the commandments of the Decalogue. Hence the tables on which the law was inscribed have been called "the tables of the covenant." Exod 19 and 20; Exod 22:15;[3] Heb 9:4.

12. **Q:** *Is the condition of works a condition of merits?*

    A: Not at all. Rather, it is one of duties that bear witness to gratitude towards God the Creator. Rom 11:35; Luke 17:10.[4]

13. **Q:** *But works of a holy and upright nature must be perfectly holy and good.*

---

3. Rollock's use of Exod 22:15 as a proof-text here appears to be in error. Presumably Exod 25:16, which refers to the tables of the covenant, was intended.

4. Rollock's teaching here, at least, subverts Holmes Rolston III's claim that Reformed theology's doctrine of the covenant of works exalted "the merit and ability of man." In Rolston's estimation, the notion of the covenant of works comprised the basic idea that "a reward is promised to man, if he earns it by his own good works." Rollock, however, explicitly denies that man in the covenant of works could properly *earn* or *merit* the reward of life proffered to him. See Rolston, "Responsible Man," 33.

A: It does not follow from this that they must be meritorious. For the rule of merit is properly this: compensation is due to work that is done—work that is not owed—according to the order of justice. As Rom 4:4 says, "To the one who works"—that is, to the one who merits—"wages are reckoned according to debt."[5]

14. **Q:** *Why is this covenant called the covenant of works?*

    A: The reason for the name is discovered in the condition of the covenant, which is works proceeding from a good and upright nature.

15. **Q:** *When was this covenant of works established with man?*

    A: It was established with man in his first creation. Gen 1:27ff.; Gen 2:15ff.

16. **Q:** *In what manner and order was it established?*

    A: First God engraved his law—that is, the heads of his covenant's condition—upon the heart of created man. Then he said, "Work and serve according to the rule of my law (for it is written upon your heart), and you will live." And man accepted the condition, and pledged himself to fulfill it. Gen 2:15ff.

17. **Q:** *You understand, then, this moral law to have been engraved upon man's heart at creation, and thus the singular heads*

---

5. Rollock's argument is that Adam's good works could not have been considered meritorious since Adam was *indebted* to God by virtue of God's goodness to him in creation. Only un-obligatory work (*opus indebitum*) can rightly be considered meritorious. Interestingly, Rollock's gloss on Romans 4:4—"Ei qui operatur, id est, ei qui meretur, merces imputatur ex debito"—closely mirrors similar glosses upon the biblical text by sixteenth-century Roman Catholic scholastic thinkers in their discussions of merit and man's initial grace in creation. So, for instance, the Spanish Dominican Bartolomé de Medina (d. 1581) notes in his commentary on Thomas's *Summa Theologiae* 1a2ae, q. 114, a. 5: ". . . dicit Paulus, Ei qui operatur, id est, ei qui meretur, merces non imputatur secundum gratiam, sed secundum debitum." Medina, *Expositio*, 1123.

The Covenant and the Sacrament

of this covenant's condition to have been known by nature itself?

A: I do. And your own lingering acquaintance with the law, which still persists in corrupted nature after the fall, is proof of this very thing. Rom 1:19 and 32; Rom 2:14.

18. **Q:** *Was this covenant of works afterwards repeated?*

    A: It was continually repeated from the creation and fall of man up until the coming of Christ. First, it was delivered by a living voice. Then, it was engraved upon tables of stone by the fingers of God himself. Afterwards, it was handed down and inscribed by Moses. Finally, it was repeated and inscribed by the Prophets, each in his own place and order. And so it is known to us from the Old Testament.[6]

19. **Q:** *In what manner and order was it repeated?*

    A: You have the order in Exodus chapters 19 and 20. First, God said though Moses, "If you will observe my covenant—that is, my law—then you will surely be a peculiar people to me." Then the people said together, "Whatever Jehovah says, we will do." When this promise of the people was related to God through Moses, God promulgated his law—that is, the heads of his covenant that the people were required to observe—from Mount Sinai.

20. **Q:** *But have you not just said that the law comes first, and the covenant follows after?*[7]

    A: It is the same whether the words of the covenant, which contain God's promise and mankind's counter-promise, precede the law—that is, the statement of the heads of the

---

6. Cf. Rollock's catechism on "the means whereby God from the beginning hath revealed both his covenants unto mankind," which concludes his *Treatise of God's Effectual Calling* (in *Works*, 1:274–88).

7. This refers back to the "manner and order" in which the covenant of works was initially established with man (q. 16).

condition comprised in God's covenant—or follow after it.

21. **Q:** *To what end was this covenant repeated with the ancient Church and people after the fall of man, since—after the fall—the condition of good works proceeding from nature was impossible to man (Rom 8:3)?*[8]

    A: Not to that particular end that men should be justified and live through it, but rather that they, convicted in their consciences and overwhelmed by the impossibility of that condition of good works of nature, might flee to the covenant of grace. Deut 10:16; Rom 3:19; Rom 7:7ff.

22. **Q:** *So you mean that the covenant of works was repeated with the ancient people especially towards the end that they might be prepared for the covenant of grace?*

    A: I do.

23. **Q:** *But not all were prepared, and not all fled to the covenant of grace.*

    A: True. But the elect were prepared. The reprobate, indeed, were reduced at length to desperation. Rom 11:7.

24. **Q:** *Was the covenant of grace also established with the ancient Church and people?*

    A: It was, albeit there was only obscure mention of it in the doctrine of the covenant of works and of the law. Gen 3:5. Gen 49:10; Gen 22:18; Gen 26:4.

25. **Q:** *Did, then, man fail with respect to the covenant of works?*

    A: He did indeed. Rom 3:4.

26. **Q:** *When did he first fail with respect to the covenant of works?*

---

8. Cf. Rollock's discussion of the fall's impact upon human nature in *Works*, 1:166–78.

A: Immediately after creation and the establishment of that covenant. Gen 3:1ff.; Rom 5:12ff.

27. Q: *Did man fail again later with respect to that covenant?*
A: When this covenant was later repeated with the people, they committed themselves to keeping the condition of the covenant, but they did not remain true to their promise, nor were they even able to do so. Exod 32:1ff.

28. Q: *What followed from man's defection and violation of the covenant?*
A: Death of two kinds: the first of the body; the second of both the body and soul. This was in accord with the threat that was added to the promise of the covenant. Gen 2:17; Gen 3:7ff.; Rom 5:12.

29. Q: *But man did not immediately die when the covenant was violated and broken.*
A: Nevertheless each kind of death, both physical and spiritual, began, and will be perfected in its own time. Man's body was made susceptible to death, and his soul lost the image of God—that is, the life of God, which is marked by sanctity, righteousness, and wisdom. Gen 3:7; 1 Cor 15:42–43; 2 Cor 5:4; Eph 2:1; Col 2:13.

30. Q: *Where did you find the doctrine of this covenant of works?*
A: In the Old Testament; that is, it has been delivered to us at length in the writings of Moses and the Prophets (the great part of which are arranged to explain the law and the covenant of works). But it is summarily comprehended in the Decalogue.

Some Questions and Answers

CONCERNING THE COVENANT OF GRACE

31. **Q:** *Did man himself, already prostrate and dead after the breaking of the covenant of works, first consider his own liberation or redemption?*

    A: He could not even imagine his own redemption. Gen 3:8ff.; 1 Cor 11:14.

32. **Q:** *How, then, was he liberated and redeemed from such death?*

    A: Only by the intervention of God's grace and mercy—which was beyond and contrary to his expectation, inasmuch as he was spiritually dead. Gen 3:8; Eph 2:1ff.; Col 2:13; Tit 3:3ff.

33. **Q:** *What was that intervening grace of God?*

    A: God gave to man a mediator, his Son Jesus Christ. Gen 3:5; Rom 8:3; Gal 4:4; 1 John 4:9.[9]

34. **Q:** *Why, then, did the Son of God not immediately appear after the fall of man, since a mediator between both God and man in one person was then necessary?*

    A: "Jesus Christ is the same yesterday, today, and forever," and Christ is that "lamb who was slain before the foundation of the world." In other words, the virtue and efficacy of the flesh and cross of Christ, who would eventually come in his own time, existed already from the beginning. Heb 13:8; Rev 13:8; 1 Cor 2:3–4.

35. **Q:** *When was the Son of God finally manifested in our flesh?*

    A: When the fullness of time had come, God sent forth his Son, born of a woman. Gal 4:4; Eph 1:10.

36. **Q:** *What duties did the mediator who was at length given by the Father perform for the redemption of man?*

---

9. Rollock's use of Gen 3:5 as a proof-text here appears to be in error. Presumably Gen 3:15, the so-called *protoevangelion*, was intended.

A: He transferred to himself man's sin, God's wrath, and both kinds of death—physical and spiritual—that man rightly should have suffered. Deut 21:23; Gal 3:13.

37. **Q:** *So our mediator, Jesus Christ, was born under the covenant of works and under the law for our sake?*

    A: For our sake he was made liable to the covenant of works and the law, in order that he might redeem those who were liable to the law. Gal 4:4–5.

38. **Q:** *Has Christ our mediator, who was born under the covenant of works and the law, fulfilled the covenant of works and the law for our sake?*

    A: He has, and this indeed in two ways.

39. **Q:** *What are these two ways?*

    A: Both by doing and by suffering. Rom 8:3 and 5; 1 Pet 2:22ff.; Gal 3:13.

40. **Q:** *Would it not have been enough for him to have done what was right and holy his entire life for our sake, without also suffering death for us?*

    A: It would not have been enough. Indeed, the entirety of even his most holy and most righteous works could not have satisfied God's justice and wrath on account of our sins. Much less could those works have merited for us the mercy of God, reconciliation, righteousness, and eternal life. Heb 9:22–23.

41. **Q:** *Why is this?*

    A: Because God's justice necessarily required the penalty of eternal death for our past violation of the covenant of works. This was in keeping with that threat which was, as we have said above, added to the promise of the covenant. Deut 27:26.[10]

---

10. See q. & a. 4.

Some Questions and Answers

42. **Q:** *Admitting that no works of ours, even the most holy and righteous ones imaginable, could satisfy God's justice and wrath once we had broken the covenant of works, I still do not see why the mediator's works—the works of one who was not only a most holy and innocent man but also God—could not satisfy God's justice and wrath.*

    A: Just as our own works could not satisfy the justice of God, neither could the works—even the most holy ones—of the mediator between God and man. For once God's justice was violated, death was of necessity required, either from the man himself who had sinned, or indeed from the mediator in his place. Only in this way could God remain both just and true. Heb 9:22–23; Rom 3:26.

43. **Q:** *I will grant to you that the mediator satisfied God's justice and wrath on account of our sins by his death and suffering. Will you grant to me, in turn, that he merited mercy and new grace from God for us by his good and holy works?*

    A: You seem to want Christ's merit and his satisfaction to be divided and attributed to his works and his passion respectively. Thus, you say that he satisfied justice and wrath by his passion, but merited for us grace and reconciliation by his good and holy works. I will not grant this to you. 1 John 1:7.

44. **Q:** *But you must admit the mediator's good and holy works to constitute some part either of his satisfaction or his merit.*

    A: I say that, properly speaking, the mediator's good and holy works do not constitute any part of his satisfaction or his merit. For everywhere in Scripture I see Christ's satisfaction and merit ascribed to his suffering and cross, not to his deeds. Rom 3:25; Rom 5:19.

45. **Q:** *So you would have it that the mediator both satisfied divine justice and merited grace only by his passion and death?*

A: Yes, I would have both satisfaction and merit properly attributed only to the death and passion of the mediator. Rom 3:25–26; Rom 5:19.

46. **Q:** *I see, then, no use for the many wonderful works which our mediator did during his entire life.*

    A: This does not follow.

47. **Q:** *What, then, would you say was their use?*

    A: I say that the holiness of the person of Christ—who is both God and man—and all the works of that holy person were the sacred foundation of his satisfaction and his merit, which satisfaction and merit themselves belong to his passion alone. 1 Pet 3:18; Heb 7:26; Heb 9:13–14.

48. **Q:** *If you are able, make this—I beg of you—a little clearer.*

    A: What I mean is this: the dignity of Christ's most holy person, and of the works accomplished by that most holy and divine person, is the reason that his passion had such virtue and efficacy. For his passion not only satisfied God's justice and wrath on account of our sins, but also merited for us new grace and mercy.

49. **Q:** *I understand. You mean that Christ, by virtue of the sanctity of both his person and his works, was made a suitable, worthy, and efficacious sacrifice—that is, a sacrifice both satisfactory, so to speak, and meritorious?*

    A: Yes. "For it was indeed fitting that we should have such a high priest, holy, innocent, unstained, separated from sinners, and exalted above the heavens." Heb 7:26.

50. **Q:** *How manifold, therefore, is the effect of Christ the mediator's death?*

    A: Twofold: first, he satisfied the wrath of God for man's sin; and second, he merited for man new grace and mercy. Rom 3:25; Rom 4:23.

Some Questions and Answers

51. **Q:** *Why did Christ's death have so great an efficacy?*
    A: First of all because of the dignity of his person—he was both God and most holy man. And secondly because of the severity of the sufferings and death that he endured at that time.

52. **Q:** *What is the principal grace which Christ has merited for man?*
    A: The grace of reconciliation with God. Rom 5:10.

53. **Q:** *How was reconciliation with God accomplished?*
    A: Reconciliation was accomplished by the establishing of a new covenant with man. Jer 31:33; Heb 8:8.

54. **Q:** *What was that new covenant?*
    A: It was that which men commonly call the covenant of grace, or the gratuitous covenant.

55. **Q:** *What is the covenant of grace?*
    A: It is the covenant in which God promises man righteousness and eternal life under the condition of faith in Christ the mediator, and man accepts the condition, and commits himself to believe. Hab 2:4; Joel 1:31; Rom 9:10; Mark 16:16.

56. **Q:** *What is the foundation of this gratuitous covenant?*
    A: First of all, the satisfactory and meritorious death of Christ; and secondly, the mercy of God, which Christ's death has merited. From this more proximate foundation—God's mercy—the covenant of grace arises. Rom 3:24.

57. **Q:** *Then the foundation of the covenant of grace differs from the foundation of the covenant of works?*
    A: Indeed, the foundations of these two covenants are entirely at odds with one another. They are as mutually contrary

as nature and grace, which can in no way cohere in the work of redemption. Rom 11:6.

58. **Q:** *What things are promised in the covenant of grace?*
    A: Righteousness and eternal life. Rom 5:21.

59. **Q:** *What is this righteousness which is promised?*
    A: It is not an inherent righteousness, the kind that was lost in Adam at the beginning. Rather it is the righteousness of God—that is, a righteousness which God imputes to man through faith; a righteousness more excellent than inherent righteousness, just as Christ was more excellent than Adam; a righteousness without which man cannot stand before God and his judgment seat. Rom 3:22; Rom 5:12ff.

60. **Q:** *What is this life which is promised?*
    A: It is the effect of Christ's imputed righteousness in us. It begins in this life as inherent holiness, and is perfected in the life to come as glory. Rom 5:21; Rom 6:22; Rom 8:30.

61. **Q:** *What is the condition of the gratuitous covenant?*
    A: The very name of the gratuitous covenant suggests either that there is no condition (for when someone promises to give something freely, he properly demands no condition), or at least that the condition of the gratuitous covenant is itself completely free—that is, a result of God's pure grace. Isa 55:1; Rom 3:24.

62. **Q:** *What is this condition which you call "free"?*
    A: Faith in the mediator. Rom 10:6; Gal 3:14.

63. **Q:** *Does faith, then, spring from grace?*
    A: Yes indeed. It is entirely of grace, not of man's natural powers. Phil 1:29.[11]

---

11. See *Works*, 1:40. Rollock's identification of faith—that "condition" which the individual performs in the covenant of grace—as God's free gift to

Some Questions and Answers

64. **Q:** *Does, then, this condition of faith in Christ and God's mercy exclude, in and of itself, those good works of nature that were named as the condition of the covenant of works?*

    A: It completely excludes them. For Christ and God's mercy, which are the objects of faith, cannot—in the justification of man—consist with the powers of man's nature or the works that proceed from that nature. Rom 3:28; Rom 11:6.

65. **Q:** *Does the condition of faith also exclude works of regeneration or of grace?*

    A: It excludes these as well. For, indeed, works of regeneration cannot claim even so much as some portion of the reason or merit that man should be justified and saved. Rom 4:2–3; Phil 3:8.

66. **Q:** *You wish, then, faith alone—that is, Christ alone apprehended by faith—to constitute the condition of the gratuitous covenant?*

    A: I do. For that which is the condition in the gratuitous covenant is equally the reason for man's justification—the reason, that is, for the fulfilment of the promise in the covenant of grace. But faith alone—that is, Christ alone apprehended by faith—justifies. Therefore faith alone is the condition of the gratuitous covenant. Rom 4:13ff.

67. **Q:** *So you wish the condition of the gratuitous covenant and the reason that God should fulfill the promise of the gratuitous*

---

the elect serves to illustrate the compatibility of covenant theology (and its inherent emphasis upon reciprocal obligations for both parties) with the traditional predestinarian bent of Reformed theology. Some historians of Reformed covenant theology have (wrongly) treated Reformed covenant theology as if it served to counterbalance the predestinarian emphasis of sixteenth-century Reformed teaching (Cf. Miller, *Errand*, 43–98; Baker, *Bullinger and the Covenant*, 199–200; 205–7). Against the notion that covenant theology and traditional Reformed predestinarian teaching stood in tension if not simple contradiction to one another, see Muller, "Covenant of Works," 87.

The Covenant and the Sacrament

covenant—that is, the reason that God should actually justify us according to the terms of his covenant—to be one and the same thing?

A: I do. Indeed, these three things are truly one and the same in this covenant: the foundation of the gratuitous covenant; the condition of the covenant; and the reason that God fulfills the promise of the covenant unto us. For Christ crucified is the foundation of the gratuitous covenant, the condition of the covenant, and the reason for the fulfilment of the thing promised in the covenant. Gal 3:8–9; 2 Cor 1:20.

68. **Q:** *Is there no difference between these three things?*

    A: They only differ in our reckoning: for as the foundation of the covenant, Christ crucified is considered absolutely; as the condition of the covenant, he is considered as one who must be apprehended by faith (for a condition is something which belongs to the future, something which is yet to be fulfilled); as, finally, the reason that God should fulfil the promise of the covenant, he is considered as one already apprehended by faith in time past. Rom 3:24 and 28.

69. **Q:** *Would there, then, be anything in the covenant of grace, were it not for merit?*

    A: Nothing. For the covenant itself is founded upon merit, and the promise of the covenant is established under the condition of merit, and the reason, finally, that the promise should be fulfilled has been merited. Heb 9:15ff; 2 Cor 1:20; Gal 3:17; Rom 4:1; Rom 10:9–10.

70. **Q:** *How, therefore, can you call the covenant gratuitous, since grace and merit greatly disagree?*

    A: Because the merit in question belongs entirely to Christ the mediator; the covenant is entirely free with respect to us. The covenant is called "gratuitous" by virtue of its being free to us, not by virtue of its being free to Christ. Rom 3:24; Rom 4:16.

71. **Q:** *Of what use, then, are works of regeneration, if they neither form any part of the condition which is in the gratuitous covenant, nor any part of the reason for our justification and salvation?*

    A: They exist in order that we might thank God for our calling—which calling exists by means of the gratuitous covenant established with us—and for our justification. 2 Cor 5:15; Eph 4:1.

72. **Q:** *But throughout Scripture you find the reward of eternal life promised on condition of works of holiness. Do these promises not belong to the gratuitous covenant? And if they do, does it not follow that works of regeneration constitute some part, at least, of that condition which belongs to the gratuitous covenant?*

    A: These promises belong neither to the gratuitous covenant nor to the covenant of works.

73. **Q:** *Why not?*

    A: Because the promise of the covenant of works, repeated after the fall, was to man not yet justified or renewed. So also was the promise of the gratuitous covenant. These promises are made to man already justified and renewed. Rom 3:23–24; 1 Tim 4:8.

74. **Q:** *To what end are these promises made to men already justified and renewed?*

    A: To the end that men already justified and renewed might be stirred up, by the display of the reward of eternal life, to works of regeneration. 1 Tim 4:8; Gal 6:9.

75. **Q:** *Then you would have three distinct kinds of promise be found in Sacred Scripture, and especially in the New Testament?*

A: I would.

76. **Q:** *What are these?*

A: The first is the promises of the covenant of works. The second is those of the gratuitous covenant. The third is those promises made with men already called, justified, and renewed. By this third kind of promise men are stirred up unto duties of gratitude towards God the redeemer, which duties are discovered in that part of the doctrine of the gospel which concerns holiness of life and good morals. You see this third kind of promise interspersed among those exhortations and precepts which have been delivered concerning a holy life.

77. **Q:** *What, then, are the heads of that condition which belongs to the gratuitous covenant?*

A: Those things that should be believed (for we can call such the heads of the condition) concerning God, concerning Christ the mediator, and concerning his benefits. These things are fully set forth in the gospel, and are comprehended in a few words in that which is called the Apostles' Creed.

78. **Q:** *Why is this covenant called "gratuitous"?*

A: Because the condition of the covenant is nothing, or is at least entirely free.

79. **Q:** *When was this gratuitous covenant first established with man?*

A: It was established immediately after the fall of man. Gen 3:5.[12]

---

12. Here, and again in q. & a. 80, Gen 3:15 rather than Gen 3:5 is presumably intended.

Some Questions and Answers

80. **Q:** *Was it at that time established with many words?*

    A: No. In the beginning, rather, a certain obscure promise of the Seed of the Woman—that is, of Christ and his benefits—was made. Gen 3:5.

81. **Q:** *Was this gratuitous covenant repeated afterwards?*

    A: It was continually repeated from the fall of man up until the manifestation of Christ, at which time it began, at last, to be expressed very clearly and openly. Indeed, at that time it began to be said: "Whoever believes in Christ crucified will be justified and live." John 3:18; Rom 10:9–10.

82. **Q:** *Is, therefore, the substance of that covenant of grace which was established with the ancient people, and of this covenant of grace which is established with Christ's Church at the time of his advent, one and the same?*

    A: They are the same in thing and substance, but diverse in accidents. By virtue of such diversity in accidents, that one is called the old covenant or testament, while this one is called the new covenant or testament. Heb 8:8ff.

83. **Q:** *So by the name "Old Testament" you understand the covenant of grace?*

    A: The name "Old Testament" broadly extends to both the law, or covenant of works, and to the covenant of grace which was joined to the law. The Apostle, writing to the Hebrews, teaches that the term "Old Testament" should be accepted thus. Heb 8 and 9.

84. **Q:** *Then the covenant of grace established with that ancient people is also called the Old Testament?*

    A: It is.

85. **Q:** *What order did the Apostles observe in promulgating this gratuitous covenant after Christ's manifestation and his ascension into heaven?*

A: First, they preached the gospel—that is, they proclaimed, first of all, Christ humiliated, and then Christ glorified, and thirdly and finally they taught the benefits which flow from his death and his glory. Then, they concluded their gospel with this promise: "Whoever believes in this Christ—first humiliated thus, then glorified—will be made a sharer in Christ and all of his benefits." In these words we have the gratuitous covenant. Acts 2:14ff.

86. **Q:** *Was this gratuitous covenant never at any time clearly and expressly set forth and explained before Christ's manifestation in the flesh?*

    A: It was never so clearly set forth before Christ's advent as it was after his coming. Yet it cannot be denied that, long before Christ's advent, this covenant was revealed rather clearly by the Patriarchs and Prophets, and that the latest of the Prophets spoke about it with even greater clarity. Heb 1:1; 1 John 1:18; 2 Peter 1:19.

87. **Q:** *Who at length among the Prophets spoke most clearly about the covenant?*

    A: Paul quotes that which is said by the Prophet Habakkuk, "The righteous will live by faith," in Rom 1:17. He likewise quotes the Prophet Joel, "Whoever believes in him will not be made ashamed," in Rom 10:11. With these words we have at least the outline of the gratuitous covenant. According to Paul's witness, then, these two Prophets spoke of the gratuitous covenant most clearly.

88. **Q:** *To what end was this covenant repeated?*

    A: To the same end, clearly, for which it was first established with man immediately after the fall—namely, that man should be justified through faith and should live. Jer 31:33; Heb 8:8.

Some Questions and Answers

89. **Q:** *So you would have the reason for this covenant's repetition differ from that for the repetition of the covenant of works?*

    A: I would. For as we have seen above, the covenant of works was not repeated with man with the same specific purpose for which it was first established.

90. **Q:** *What if man, after breaking the covenant of works, should not accept the condition of this gratuitous covenant?*

    A: Then surely he could never be justified and saved. John 3:18; Mark 16:16.

91. **Q:** *Did the first man believe, in accordance with the condition of the gratuitous covenant, both for himself and his posterity?*

    A: The covenant was indeed established with Adam and his posterity or seed. But faith and grace in Christ are not propagated to posterity in the way that some goods or evils flow to children by nature. Gen 5:3; Gen 17:7; Rom 5:12; Phil 1:20.

92. **Q:** *What if someone has committed himself to believe, and has begun to believe, and to have his mind illumined, and to taste in his heart the good word of God and the virtues of the age to come—what if that one, I say, should afterwards falter and fall away from God?*

    A: Such a one cannot be restored anew through repentance, nor will any third covenant be established with him. Heb 6:6; Heb 12:17.

93. **Q:** *Then one who breaks this gratuitous covenant is in a worse place and condition than man was after the breaking of the first covenant of works. For there was room, in the breaking of the covenant of works, for repentance and the mercy of God in Christ. But if the covenant of grace is broken, there will be, you say, no room for repentance.*

A: In truth, the one who breaks the gratuitous covenant is in a worse place, and his sin is unpardonable, because it is a sin against the Holy Spirit. Such sin has a quality to it that requires the one who has sinned against the Holy Spirit to be so punished by God with final blindness that he is unable to earnestly and sincerely repent of his sin. Matt 12:31.

94. **Q:** *You are saying, then, that no third covenant can be established with a man when that second covenant, which is called gratuitous, has already been violated by him?*

    A: Yes. For if we continue sinning after receiving the knowledge of the truth, no further sacrifice for our sins remains, but only a horrible expectation of judgment and of fiery heat which will devour God's adversaries. Heb 10:26–27.

95. **Q:** *So a covenant cannot be renewed without a sacrifice and sacrificial victim?*

    A: God cannot be reconciled to a sinner and covenant-breaker without some sacrifice by which his justice and wrath are truly satisfied. That first covenant did not require a mediator and a sacrifice, because man was not a sinner when that covenant of works was first established with him. When that covenant of works was repeated with the people of Israel, it was not established immediately by God himself, but through the ministry of the messenger Moses. This was evidence of God's disagreement with the people on account of their sins. Gal 3:19. The second covenant—that which we call gratuitous—had need of both a mediator and a sacrifice, because man had sinned, and sin is not expiated without a sacrifice: "For without the shedding of blood there is no remission of sins." Heb 9:22. If man should now fall from this second covenant, there can be no remission of his sin, nor should a third covenant be sought, because no further sacrifice can be found.

Some Questions and Answers

96. **Q:** *But if someone falls from this covenant of grace (for you seem to be saying that someone can fall from it), does it not follow that faith in Christ, the Holy Spirit, and grace once received can be lost, even though the Apostle says in Rom 11:29 that the gifts of God in Christ are of such a kind that one cannot repent of them?*

    A: In our reckoning there are two kinds of faith: one which men call temporary and hypocritical; the other perpetual, which men also call *anypokriton* [ἀνυπόκριτον]—that is, unfeigned.[13] Temporary and hypocritical faith, because it is only superficial and is not deeply rooted in the heart, can be entirely lost. But perpetual and unfeigned faith, because it is not superficial, but is deeply rooted in the heart, can never be entirely plucked up or removed from the heart. Therefore, one who has received the gift of unfeigned faith cannot fall away entirely from God's covenant, nor can he fall into that sin which they call the sin against the Holy Spirit. 1 John 3:9; Luke 19:26; John 10:28.

97. **Q:** *Has the covenant of works been abolished for those who are now under the covenant of grace?*

    A: It has been abolished as a means unto justification or condemnation. But it still has some use to believers as a means unto conversion, faith, regeneration, and the mortification of the flesh. Gal 3:13; Gal 4:5; Rom 3:31; Rom 6:15; Rom 7:4ff.

98. **Q:** *Can you explain this?*

    A: Yes. First of all, those who are in Christ are justified and saved by faith in Christ alone, not by works of the law. Rom 3:28. There is no condemnation unto those who are in Christ, for Christ was made a curse for them. Gal 3:13. Secondly, however, those who are in Christ—since they do not perfectly believe and are not perfectly converted

---

13. Rollock transliterates the Greek adjective in its feminine accusative form (*anypokriton*) to agree with the case and gender of the Latin *fidem*.

or perfectly renewed (Rom 7:18)—have lasting need of those terrors of the covenant of works, that they might be goaded to make constant progress in their faith, conversion, and sanctification.

99. **Q:** *Has that moral law, which contained the heads of that condition which was required in the covenant of works, likewise been abrogated when the covenant of works was abolished?*

    A: Inasmuch as the moral law serves the interests of the covenant of works, the same reasoning plainly applies to it as to the covenant of works: it is abolished insofar as the covenant of works is abolished; it continues insofar as the covenant of works continues.

100. **Q:** *Can the moral law be considered in some regard other than its relation to the covenant of works—that is, in some regard other than its role in comprising the heads of the condition of the covenant of works?*

    A: It can.

101. **Q:** *How?*

    A: After the advent of Christ the moral law began to openly serve the interests of the covenant of grace, and to contain the heads and rules of Christian duties, and of works not now of nature but of grace and regeneration. Thus the moral law endures, because it serves and ministers in some way within the covenant of grace itself; it endures, I say, not now inscribed upon tables of stone, but upon the tables of hearts of flesh. Jer 31:33; Rom 3:31; 2 Cor 3:2.

102. **Q:** *Where, finally, is the doctrine of this covenant that you call gratuitous found?*

    A: In each Testament, both Old and New, although it is delivered more clearly and fully in the New Testament and the writings of the Apostles. Moreover, a short summary of the doctrine of this covenant is comprehended in that statement which men commonly call the Apostles' Creed.

Thus far concerning the gratuitous covenant of God

CONCERNING THE SACRAMENT IN GENERAL

103. **Q:** *Has God sealed his covenant, whether the covenant of works or the covenant of grace, with a sacrament—that is, with his seal?*

    A: He has indeed sealed each of his covenants with a sacrament, as if with his own seal. Gen 2:9; Gen 17:11; Rom 4:11.

104. **Q:** *Will you describe to me the manner in which he sealed, first of all, that covenant of works?*

    A: He sealed the covenant of works in this manner, and in this, as it were, preserved form. The words of the covenant were set forth in this fashion: "Are you willing," God said to the man, "to work well and fulfill my law, so that you might live?" The man answered, "I am willing." God replied, "Upon that condition and according to that law, I promise you truly eternal life. And, that this might be more certain to you, I seal this covenant of mine to you with my very own seal." Then God presented his seal and sacrament. Gen 2:15–17; Gen 17:11; Rom 4:11; Rev 2:7.

105. **Q:** *By what sacrament did he seal that covenant of works?*

    A: The trees of that Garden of Eden were, without a doubt, the very sacraments and seals of God's covenant. There was that tree of the knowledge of good and evil, and there was the tree of life. Gen 2:9; Gen 3:22.

106. **Q:** *In what manner and fashion was the covenant of grace sealed?*

The Covenant and the Sacrament

A: The same fashion, clearly, in which the covenant of works was sealed. God said, "Are you willing to believe in Christ the mediator?" Man answered, "I am willing." Then God said, "Upon that law and condition, I will justify you and will give you eternal life. And, that you might believe this even more, I seal this promise of mine to you with my own seal or sacrament." Gen 1:11; Acts 8:37–38.

107. **Q:** *By what sacraments did God then seal—and even now does seal—his covenant of grace?*

A: By various sacraments from the beginning until now. Gen 2:9. Gen 17:11; Exod 12:1ff.; 1 Cor 10:1ff.

108. **Q:** *Since the Word of God alone, without seal or sacrament, is firm and unchangeable as such (for God is not a man that he should lie, as Num 23:19 says), why was a seal added to his word and to the promise established in the covenant, as if his word required some seal to make it stronger—as if, in truth, his word were not sufficiently firm and certain in and of itself?*

A: A seal was added to God's word and promise not for God's sake, nor for that of his word, which truly—if considered in itself and with regard to its own strength and certitude—was able to provide for man on its own, without a sacrament. It was added, rather, for the sake of man, who is weak by nature, and whose faith needed the support of the sacraments. Rom 3:4; Rom 4:11; Heb 6:17–18.

109. **Q:** *Did then man in creation—before the fall, when he existed in the state of innocence—labor under such infirmity, and require these supports for the building up of his faith?*

A: Created man was, to be sure, without sin, but he was not without any weakness or mutability of nature. Man was, in his first creation, liable to change. Thus, to make him firm in his faith, so that he would not be moved, God gave man his sacrament together with the word of the covenant. Jas 1:13; Job 4:18; Job 15:13; Matt 19:17.

110. **Q:** *In light of man's infirmity—or rather, in truth, his infidelity—after the fall, is there any question why God, since man has need, should have added his seal or sacrament to his covenant?*

A: There is no question. Rom 3:10; Rom 3:23; Gen 6:5.

111. **Q:** *Is there, then, some degree of faithlessness mixed with the faith that man enjoys in this life?*

A: There is. 1 Cor 13:9; Eph 3:19; Col 1:9.

112. **Q:** *Setting aside those ancient sacraments, both of the covenant of works and of the covenant of grace, will you tell me something about those sacraments of the covenant of grace and the New Testament that were instituted by Christ at his coming?*

A: I will teach you at present some things about the sacraments in general, which—when well understood—will render more specific doctrine about both baptism and the Lord's Supper easy to receive.

113. **Q:** *Where will you begin with this general doctrine concerning the sacraments of the New Testament?*

A: I will begin by discussing those things that are signified in a sacrament.

114. **Q:** *How many things in general, then, are signified?*

A: The whole of what is signified in the sacraments can be reduced to four things. The first thing signified is Christ himself, who is both God and man. The second is the cross or passion of Christ. The third is the benefits flowing from Christ's passion, such as the forgiveness of sins, justification, the gift of the Holy Spirit, regeneration, and eternal life. The fourth thing signified is the inward application

The Covenant and the Sacrament

of, first of all, Christ, and then of his cross, and finally of his benefits to men. Rom 6:3; Gal 3:26–27; Rom 4:11; 1 Cor 10:4; 1 Cor 11:24; Acts 2:38.

115. **Q:** *In order that we might now proceed from the things signified to the sacramental signs, I ask you, first of all, what you identify as "signs" with regard to a sacrament?*

A: I identify as "signs" not only the elements themselves, but also the rites and whatever outward actions are involved in the sacrament. 1 Cor 11:23–26.

116. **Q:** *Will you tell me what the signs in each sacrament—both baptism and the Lord's Supper—are, and which of those spiritual realities numbered above each sign signifies?*

A: I will.

117. **Q:** *Then let us begin with baptism: what in baptism is the sign of Christ himself and the substance (so to speak) of his blood?*

A: The sign of Christ and the substance of his blood is the water. Matt 3:11; John 1:33; John 3:5.

118. **Q:** *And what in baptism is the sign of Christ's cross or passion?*

A: The pouring of the water, which signifies the effusion of God's blood. Isa 44:1–3.

119. **Q:** *And what in baptism is the sign of those benefits which flow from Christ's passion?*

A: The sign of Christ's passion and of those benefits is the same; namely, the pouring of the water.

120. **Q:** *And finally, what in baptism is the sign of the application of those three spiritual realities?*[14]

A: There is one single sign of the application of those three spiritual realities; namely, the sprinkling or pouring of

---

14. Namely, Christ, his cross, and his benefits (see q. & a. 114).

water, by means of which water is externally applied to the one who is baptized, in order to wash that one. Heb 12:24; 1 Pet 1:2; Tit 3:5; Acts 22:16.

121. **Q:** *You have spoken about the signs existing in baptism of those spiritual realities signified by the sacraments. Will you now speak about the signs of those same realities as they exist in the Lord's Supper?*
A: I will.

122. **Q:** *Then I ask: What in the Lord's Supper are the signs of Christ himself, his body, and his blood?*
A: The bread and the wine. Matt 26:6ff.; Mark 14:22ff.; Luke 22:19ff.; 1 Cor 10:16ff.; 1 Cor 11.23ff.

123. **Q:** *What in the Lord's Supper are the signs of Christ's cross and passion?*
A: The breaking of the bread, and the pouring of the wine. Matt 26:6ff.; Mark 14:22ff.; Luke 22:19ff.; 1 Cor 10:16ff.; 1 Cor 11.23ff.

124. **Q:** *What in the Lord's Supper are the signs of Christ's benefits?*
A: They are the same as those of his passion; namely, the breaking of bread, and the pouring of wine.

125. **Q:** *Finally, what in the Lord's Supper are the signs of the application of those three spiritual realities?*[15]
A: There are several signs of this application, each one individually signifying the application of all three of those spiritual realities at once. These are: 1) The giving of the bread and wine on the part of the minister; 2) The receiving of the same on the part of the people; 3) The eating of the bread on the part of the people; and 4) the drinking of the wine on the part of the people. Matt 26.6ff.; Mark 14.22ff.; Luke 22.19ff.; 1 Cor 10.16ff.; 1 Cor 11.23ff.

---

15. See previous note.

The Covenant and the Sacrament

126. **Q:** *Based on what you have said about the signs of the sacraments, I observe, first of all, that in each sacrament the sign of the passion or cross and the sign of Christ's benefits is one and the same.*

    A: You observe correctly. And this is because the benefits of Christ all flow from his passion. 1 John 1:7.

127. **Q:** *I observe, secondly, that in each sacrament one and the same sign signifies the application of all three of those spiritual realities at once.*

    A: And this too you observe correctly. For the application of Christ, his cross, and his benefits is one and the same work. Gal 3:26ff.; Rom 8:32.

128. **Q:** *I understand now what the signs are in each sacrament, and what spiritual reality each sign signifies. I wish now to learn from you whether or not these signs are naked and idle?*

    A: They are not. Rather, these signs effectually accomplish something, and are organs and instruments of the Holy Spirit. Rom 4:12; Rom 6:4; Tit 3:5.

129. **Q:** *Will you explain this to me?*

    A: I will. In each sacrament there are, indeed, signs of Christ, his cross, and his benefits—signs, that is, of those very heavenly realities which are not yet applied to us. But these signs are also instruments of the Holy Spirit, by which he illumines our minds and effectually works in us understanding of those spiritual realities, which understanding is the first part of faith. Rom 4:11.

130. **Q:** *And what about the signs of the application of those spiritual realities in each sacrament?*[16]

    A: These too are instruments of the Holy Spirit, by which he not only works understanding in our minds, which is

---

16. See q. & a. 114.

the first part of faith, but also works within our hearts a more intimate application; that is, he works that very reality which the signs signify—the understanding of which reality he has first created in our minds. And this more intimate application is truly the second part of faith. Rom 4:11; Gal 3:27.[17]

131. **Q:** *Then it is with reference to these signs of the application of those spiritual realities that the sacraments are called exhibiting, applying, conferring signs and* sphragides [σφραγίδες] *or "seals"—for they are commonly called by such names?*

A: It is. Indeed, sacraments are signs of the application of those spiritual realities, through which the Holy Spirit not only works understanding, which is of the mind, but also application, which is of the heart, and through which the Spirit presents to us Christ, his cross, and his benefits. Rom 4:11.[18]

132. **Q:** *Thus far you have discussed, first of all, the realities signified by the sacraments, and then the signs of the sacraments. I would now learn from you the reasons that these signs which you identify in each sacrament should represent those heavenly realities signified, and so be signs of them,*

---

17. Cf. Rollock's discussion of the "parts" of faith in *Works*, 1:182–86.

18. Rollock's repeated use of the term *applicatio* here might lend itself to confusion. Read in conjunction with his comments on the sacraments in his Romans commentary (see "On the Sacrament" below), it seems clear that Rollock's first use of application in this answer—"application of those spiritual realities"—refers to God's application of Christ and his benefits to believers (which application is represented as such in each sacrament). The second use refers to the believer's *apprehension* of Christ—that is, the believer's laying hold of Christ (and his benefits) through true faith. In his Romans commentary Rollock uses the term *apprehensio* to name this second fruit of the Spirit's work in believers—above and beyond intellectual illumination—by means of the sacraments. I have rendered both uses of *applicatio* in this answer with the word's most obvious English derivative ("application"). Perhaps, however, the second use of the term would be better rendered "joining" or "uniting."

The Covenant and the Sacrament

and should bring about, as instruments of the Holy Spirit, understanding and application of them.

A: This will in no part be lacking to you.

133. **Q:** *Therefore how many reasons are there that those sacramental signs should represent the realities they signify and effect understanding as well as application of those realities?*

    A: There are two reasons. The first is the analogy and symmetry between the signs and the things signified. The second is the spiritual or supernatural relation between signs and things signified—from which there arises that union which is called "sacramental." 1 Cor 10:16–17; 1 Pet 3:22.

134. **Q:** *Will you explain to me that which you have called analogy or symmetry.*

    A: Analogy or symmetry arises from a certain natural quality of that thing which is a sign. By virtue of this quality the thing which is a sign resembles that reality which it signifies. In baptism, for example, there is similarity between water and the blood of the Lord, because water has a natural quality—namely, its aptitude for washing or purifying dirty bodies—that makes it similar to the blood of the Lord, by which our spiritual dirtiness is washed away. In the Lord's Supper, likewise, there is an analogy and symmetry between the bread and the Lord's body, since bread has a quality—namely, its aptitude for feeding and nourishing one's physical life—that makes it similar to the body of the Lord, by which we are nourished unto eternal life. The same judgment applies to the rest of the signs in every sacrament. For in each there is an analogy or symmetry between those things which are signs and those realities which are signified. John 8:12; 1 Cor 10:16–17.

135. **Q:** *Is this analogy or symmetry existing between signs and realities signified so necessary that without it these things could not signify or represent those spiritual realities?*

Some Questions and Answers

A: It is. For if no analogy or symmetry should exist between some sign and some reality signified, then that sign could not be a sign of the reality. For example, a stone cannot be a sign of a man, since there is no analogy or symmetry between a stone and a man.

136. **Q:** *You have spoken about analogy. I would now that you might say something about that second reason which you mentioned for the signification and effectiveness of the signs in sacraments—namely, that spiritual relation.*

    A: I will say something also about this.

137. **Q:** *What, therefore, do you say about this spiritual relation?*

    A: By virtue of this spiritual relation, no sooner is some sacramental sign presented to one's physical eyes than the spiritual reality signified is displayed to the mind and the eyes of faith. Indeed, there exists such a quality between these two related things—sign and spiritual reality signified—that one cannot be recognized without the other immediately springing to mind. So in Gen 17:11, Rom 4:11, and Ez. 20:12, reference is made only to the sign or seal because the sign stands in this relation to the spiritual reality.

138. **Q:** *From whence arises this relation that you call "spiritual"?*

    A: Not, to be sure, from the nature of the sign itself, from whence we have said that the relationship of analogy arises. This spiritual relation arises, in truth, from the Lord's own institution and promise, and from the prayers of our Lord joined to the same. Indeed, by means of the Lord's institution, this thing which is a sign is transferred from common to sacred use, and so made a sacrament—that is, a sign which is both related to a spiritual and heavenly reality (in order to signify that reality) and sacramentally united with that reality. Thus, for example, by virtue of the

Lord's institution, the water of baptism now represents his own blood, and so has been made a sacrament of the Lord's blood. 1 Cor 11:23ff.; Rom 4:17.

139. **Q:** *Then you would not have analogy alone establish something as a sacramental sign?*

A: I would not. For it is not the case that whatever is analogous to a particular thing by virtue of some similarity to it immediately becomes a sign of that thing. To be a true sign of something, a certain institution or ordination—either of God or of man—is required. Otherwise, of course, all bread would be a sign and sacrament of the Lord's body, since there is no bread which is not comparable to the Lord's body by virtue of a certain similarity. John 6:55; 1 Tim. 4:4–5.

140. **Q:** *Then you consider this spiritual relation so necessary that without it something is not a sacrament?*

A: I do. For nothing can be a sign of a spiritual reality unless it has this relation to whatever reality is signified. Indeed, a true sign always possesses this spiritual relation to that which it signifies.

141. **Q:** *Since this relation which makes a sign or sacrament springs from the institution of God and of Christ—which institution men call the consecration—I want to know how the sacrament was instituted.*

A: The Lord, having already given thanks, pronounced the words of institution, in which he explained the use of those external things (for example, the use of the water which is in baptism, and that of the bread and wine which are in the Lord's Supper). When, then, the Lord says with regard to the Supper, "This is my body," the sense is, "This bread is the sign or sacrament of my body, and has now the role of representing my body, because I thus wish and institute it to be so." 1 Cor 11.23ff.

Some Questions and Answers

142. **Q:** *Then you would have the institutor and consecrator of the sacrament—that is, the architect of the sacrament, who transfers an element from common to sacred use—to be the Lord himself?*

    A: I would. Christ first consecrated the sacrament as such in the Last Supper. Now, however, he commonly does this same thing through men—not, indeed, through any men whatsoever without discrimination, but through those who are legitimately called; that is, through his pastors and ministers. Otherwise, indeed, there is no sacrament, but the profaning of the sacrament. Matt 28:19.

143. **Q:** *Should we consider this change of a thing from profane to sacred use, by which change a sacrament is established—should we, I say, consider this some mild change?*

    A: Certainly not. It is a great change—one which cannot be accomplished by a creature. For surely it is by virtue of this change that the thing which is changed should not only represent but also should offer and perform and even perfect in our hearts that very reality which is represented.

144. **Q:** *Do you attribute metonymical phrases, according to which external things are spoken of with reference to internal realities and vice versa, to this change to the sign and to this sacramental union, as it called?*

    A: Such common and metonymical ways of speaking arise from this very change and sacramental union, concerning which expressions see Titus 3:5, 1 Cor 10:17, and other places throughout Scripture.

145. **Q:** *You have explained to me now why the signs in each individual sacrament both signify as signs and work as instruments. Now I desire to hear from you how a sacrament differs from a word. For the word of the covenant or gospel both signifies, as a sign, and effects, as an instrument, the*

spiritual and heavenly realities in question. Indeed, the word of the gospel concerns Christ, his passion, his benefits, and the application of those very realities. And it proclaims these things not only as a sign representing or signifying them, but also as an organ and instrument of the Holy Spirit, effectually working them in our minds and our hearts. It seems to me, therefore, that word and sacrament differ not at all in function.

A: The difference is this, that a sacrament joined to the word signifies those heavenly and spiritual realities to a greater extent, and accomplishes the understanding and application of those things in our minds and hearts to a greater extent, than the word alone. Gen 17:11; Rom 4:11.

146. **Q:** *Why do you say that a sacrament added to the word signifies and works to a greater extent than the word by itself?*

A: Because while the word by itself manifests those spiritual realities only to our ears, the sacrament added to the word manifests those same realities to our eyes also. This is to say nothing about the other senses, nor about the fact that the sacrament is offered not to everyone collectively, as the word is, but even to each believer individually. Acts 2:38.

147. **Q:** *Then you would have the sacrament to differ from the word in this only, that the sacrament added to the word signifies and works to a greater extent than the word by itself?*

A: In this particular use that pertains to a sacrament—which is signifying and working—the sacrament differs from the word considered on its own only according to degree (as they say). But there is a certain further, latter use of the sacrament, arising from this former one, which properly and principally belongs in truth to the sacrament, and is in no way shared with the word. Rom 4:11.

Some Questions and Answers

148. Q: *Thus far concerning the difference between the sacrament and the word. I ask you, now, how manifold you make the use of the sacrament?*
A: It is twofold.

149. Q: *What, then, is the first use of the sacrament?*
A: It is that by which the sacrament, added to the word, signifies—insofar as it is a sign—those heavenly and spiritual realities to a greater extent and more fully than the word by itself. And, insofar as it is an instrument, it effects to a greater extent understanding of those same realities in our minds and genuine application of them—that is, *koinonian* [κοινωνίαν], or that which is commonly called "communion"—in our hearts. Rom 6:3; Gal 3:26; 1 Cor 10:16.

150. Q: *What is the second use of the sacrament?*
A: It is that by which the sacrament, added to the word, while it signifies and works to a greater extent than the word by itself, confirms to us the word of the covenant and the gospel, and aids and increases our faith in the word of the gospel, just as the seal added to an official letter increases one's confidence in that letter. And this is the principle use of the sacrament. Gen 17:11; Rom 4:11; Matt 26:28.

151. Q: *From this latter end it appears that the sacrament serves the word of the covenant, and has been ordained and instituted by the Lord for its sake, and that, hence, the word of the covenant or gospel is the primary and principal instrument by which the Holy Spirit effects faith in our hearts, and the sacrament is truly no more than a secondary and inferior organ of the Holy Spirit. Matt 28:19–20; Rom 10:8 and 17.*
A: Indeed, so it is.

152. Q: *This latter end which you have spoken about remains doubtful to me. For in regard to the gratuitous covenant,* *you have said that the covenant was ratified and established by the blood of Christ the mediator, and upon that same blood, as its foundation, was built. Now, however, in dealing with the latter end of the sacrament you say that this same gratuitous covenant is confirmed by the sacrament. Hence, you seem to me to want to say that the word of the covenant is established and ratified by both Christ's sacrifice and the sacrament.*

A: It is one thing for this covenant or Testament to be simply established, ratified, and made firm, and another thing, in truth, for our faith in the same to be confirmed, which is the ultimate and proper goal of the Testament. For the covenant of God was ratified by the mediator's sacrifice and blood alone, and on that alone has it been founded. But, in truth, our faith—so weak and infirm—in that word of the covenant is confirmed, and so enlarged, by the sacrament, as if by a sacred oath and seal of God. Let me say this more clearly: the sacrifice of Christ our mediator is, so to speak, the satisfactory and likewise meritorious cause that moved and impelled God to establish this gratuitous covenant with sinful man. The sacrament, in truth, is a certain cause, furnished by God himself, which makes man believe to a greater extent in the promise of God's covenant. "This cup is the New Testament through my blood"—that is, the sign of the new covenant that is established through my blood. 1 Cor 11:25.

153. **Q:** *I grasp the distinction. I understand also what you have said about the realities signified in the sacrament, about the signs, about the reasons that the signs signify those spiritual realities and, equally, effect understanding and application of the same, about the difference between the sacrament and the word which pertains to the sacrament's use, and about, finally, the twofold end of the sacrament. Will you now do me the favor of setting forth the sacrament in a general definition of your own, or some brief description?*

A: If you understand those two ends of a sacrament which I have related, you have your definition. For I define a sacrament in this way, according to that twofold end.

154. **Q:** *What, then, is a sacrament?*

    A: It is a sign instituted by God, effectually working, visible, through which—when it is added to the word of the gospel—the Holy Spirit represents to us to a greater extent those spiritual and heavenly realities, and effects to a greater extent than by the word alone the understanding of those realities in our minds and, in truth, the application of them in our hearts. And while he does this, the Spirit confirms our faith in the word of the covenant and gospel, and brings it to pass that we believe in that word more and more.

155. **Q:** *What is the genus in this definition?*

    A: The genus is sign.

156. **Q:** *What is the first distinction of a sacrament from other signs?*

    A: It is that this sign exists because of the institution and ordination of God, which distinguishes the sacrament from all common and profane signs whatsoever.

157. **Q:** *What is the second distinction?*

    A: It is that this sign is an effectually working instrument of the Spirit, which distinguishes a sacrament from all ineffectual signs whatsoever.

158. **Q:** *What is the third distinction?*

    A: That it is a visible sign, by which it is distinguished from the word of the gospel or covenant, which is an audible sign.

159. **Q:** *What is the fourth distinction?*
A: That which is assumed from the first end of the sacrament.

160. **Q:** *What is the fifth?*
A: That which is assumed from the latter and principal end of the sacrament.

161. **Q:** *I have now a definition and brief declaration of the sacrament. Now I ask about the name of the sacrament. Do you understand it as something complex and composed from both sign and reality signified at once, or as, in truth, a simple sign, not comprehending the reality signified?*
A: From the definition which I have given, it is evident that you should accept from me, with respect to a name for the sacrament, a sign that is indeed related and sacramentally united to the reality signified, but at the same time is not confused with or comprehended in that reality. Indeed, these signs thus related to realities must be described and defined by their relationship to those realities with which they are united, but they should not be confused with those realities. Gen 17:11; Rom 4:11.

162. **Q:** *I am satisfied concerning the sacraments of the New Testament in general. Will you say something now about each of them specifically?*
A: There will be room in the future for speaking about those sacraments specifically, that is, about baptism and the Lord's Supper separately. Concerning this, I only suggest at present that it should be easy to deduce those things which belong to the specific nature of each sacrament from those things which have been said about them in general.

Some Questions and Answers

163. **Q:** *I do not desire from you now any full teaching about each specific sacrament. I will gladly postpone that until some other time when there is greater opportunity. I only ask you now for brief definitions of each specific sacrament, in accordance with that general definition of "sacrament" given previously, with some words added about differences between these specific sacraments.*

    A: I will give you this that you seek.

164. **Q:** *What, then, is baptism?*

    A: It is a sacrament by which the New Testament, which has now for the first time been accepted, is confirmed to us, or by which our faith in the New Testament, which has already begun, is confirmed. Indeed, these two things are the same. Gen 17:10; Matt 28:29; John 4:1.

165. **Q:** *What is the Lord's Supper?*

    A: It is a sacrament by which the New Testament, which has for some length of time been accepted and preserved by faith, is confirmed, or by which the progress and continuation of our faith is confirmed. Indeed, these two things are the same. 1 Cor 11:25–26, 28.

166. **Q:** *From whence have these definitions been taken?*

    A: They have been taken from the latter and principal use of a sacrament in general, which is the confirming of the New Testament or word of the gospel.

167. **Q:** *Will you conclude by noting differences between these specific sacraments?*

    A: The special distinction of baptism is that by it the New Testament, heard and received by faith for the first time, is confirmed. But the special distinction of the Lord's Supper is that by it the New Testament, not as it has been received by faith for the first time, but as it has been preserved by faith for some length of time and is now known more clearly, is confirmed. By baptism the beginning of faith is confirmed. By the Lord's Supper, however, the increase and continuation of faith is confirmed.

Thus far concerning these truths about the sacrament in general

THE END

On the Covenant of God[1]

The covenant of God in general is a promise of grace under some settled condition. The legal covenant is the promise of eternal life under the condition of our own lawful works. The gratuitous covenant is the promise of both justice, which was lost through the fall, and eternal life under the condition of satisfaction made for sin; not a satisfaction made by us, but that made by Christ the mediator—which satisfaction must nevertheless be apprehended by faith.

Each covenant with man is in fact of grace, and only of grace. It is of grace that God should promise eternal life in the legal covenant; so too it is of grace that he should promise life in the Evangelical covenant. Nevertheless, in each covenant, the promise springs from grace in such a way that God's justice is upheld. Thus a condition has been added to the promise in each covenant, and this for the sake of divine justice, which necessarily requires the same. So, for instance, in the legal covenant, God's justice requires our works, and those most perfect. In the Evangelical covenant, God's justice requires satisfaction for the violation of that first covenant—not indeed a satisfaction of our own, but that of Christ, which must nevertheless be apprehended by our faith. From these considerations it follows that the condition of the new covenant is Christ's peculiar satisfaction, not considered without qualification,

---

1. Excerpted from Rollock, *Epistolam ad Romanos*, 161–63.

but rather as it must be apprehended by our faith, which faith is indeed a kind of secondary and subservient condition.

In order that we might understand this matter a bit more clearly, it should be examined in greater detail, and Christ the mediator should be discussed. Christ—indeed, Christ crucified—is called our mediator, because by his cross and by his death he stands in the middle (as it were) between sinful men and the wrath of God, which wrath has, I say, been prepared as the future punishment for man on account of his violation of that first, legal covenant. But Christ, interceding by his death, both subdues God's wrath and merits grace, because of the great dignity of his crucified person. And what he merits by his death is, in the first place, a new and revived covenant, which consists in the promise of new justice and new life. For each of these, both justice and life, were lost by a single violation of that old and legal covenant.

To be sure, it was not becoming that this promise now be made absolutely, without some condition. But it was suitable that the condition be met outside of us. And the condition could not have been anything other than that act by which justice was satisfied for the violation of that first covenant, and by which another, new covenant was procured. Of course, in a certain sense, the condition of the covenant is something different than that act, for the condition of the new covenant is Christ's satisfaction as that satisfaction must be apprehended by our faith, and such apprehension by faith is a thing subsequent in time to Christ's satisfaction as such. And thus, with regard to the condition of Christ's satisfaction, God guarantees and promises to us justice and life under the condition of Christ's satisfaction to be apprehended by our faith. Therefore we consider the very same Christ who procured for us the new covenant—we consider, I say, that very same one to be the primary condition of this new covenant; the secondary condition is, in truth, the faith and apprehension of Christ in our hearts, by which we in some way make that satisfaction our own, so long as we truly apply it to ourselves. We see, moreover, that this condition, Christ's satisfaction, comprises the principal and indeed meritorious cause [for the establishment of the covenant and its promises], not some ministerial or subservient cause, of which kind faith is.

Therefore the condition of the gratuitous covenant is one of satisfaction and, especially, merit—for God requires with regard to that condition that we in a certain manner merit, not indeed by ourselves but by another, that justice and life promised to us. It may perhaps be asked how I can call this covenant "gratuitous"—for it is, properly speaking, a gratuitous covenant, and is called so even with respect to the condition itself. I respond: if indeed that merit which God measures in fulfilment of the condition of the covenant was rooted in us, or if God were to measure only what belongs to us, then certainly the covenant could not be called gratuitous. But in truth that satisfaction and merit belong to another, namely Christ, and for his sake God freely grants them to us. And it is God also who weighs the reward, and brings the same forth from his own stores in compensation to us. So long, I say, as this is true, the gratuitous covenant necessarily stands and is rightly named. But we will speak about the covenant further in our teaching about the sacrament.

On the Sacrament[1]

The covenant of God with man is a promise under some settled condition. The covenant of God is twofold: there is the covenant of works; and the covenant of grace. The covenant of works is God's promise of eternal life under the condition of works. This covenant takes its name from its condition; namely, works proceeding from our own nature and virtues. This covenant was established with man in his first creation. And it was repeated afterwards with the people of Israel, but to this end: that they should be overwhelmed by that impossible condition of works, and should flee to the covenant of grace, which was also set forth under the law, even if somewhat obscurely (Deut 18:16–18). The doctrine of this covenant is to be found scattered throughout the Old Testament. And that which is called "the moral law" is nothing other than the rule of those works required in this covenant. Man, immediately after creation, cut himself off from this covenant of works though his own disobedience, oath-breaking, and deceit. Thus too, in accordance with that threat which was joined with the promise in the covenant of works, he became liable to each kind of death, both the first and the second. And so indeed, in keeping with that threat, man would have been punished, according to God's justice, with each kind of death if the mediator, the Son of God, had not intervened between sinful man and God the Father, full of wrath at sin. And this intervention was according to the

---

1. Excerpted from Rollock, *Epistolam ad Romanos*, 172–85.

kindness and grace of God himself. This mediator was the Lamb who was slain, even from the foundation of the world [Rev 13:8]; in other words, the mediator was crucified in virtue and efficacy already from the beginning of the world, even if in actual fact and time he was manifested in our nature and crucified much later, indeed in his own time.

Thus the mediator, the Son of God, bore upon his own shoulders that first defection, along with all our other sins and transgressions, simultaneously taking upon himself the wrath of God the Father which justly followed upon our sins, and making full and perfect satisfaction for us by his passion and his cross. Nor did he merely satisfy, by means of his passion, the Father's wrath and justice, but he also by that same passion—which was possible because of the dignity of him who suffered; namely, the Son of God in human nature—by that same passion, I say, he merited for us new grace. And he specifically merited the renovation of the covenant of God, without which renovation no further grace could come to us from God. For we are neither justified nor glorified unless we are first called [Rom 8:30]. But calling consists in the establishment of a new covenant with us. And this new covenant is that which we have called the covenant of grace.

The covenant of grace is God's promise of justice and eternal life under the condition of our faith in the mediator. This justice promised in this covenant is not, to be sure, the kind of justice that inheres in a man, but the kind that must be imputed to us in Christ. The justice promised, therefore, is nothing other than the righteousness of Christ himself imputed to us. The covenant of grace takes its name from that condition which belongs to it, namely, faith in the mediator. For this condition is entirely free. I explain the condition in the covenant of grace in this way: the condition in the covenant of grace is, properly speaking, Christ's cross and satisfaction, but this must be applied to us through faith. Moreover, God delivers and fulfils that which he promises in the covenant of grace, not indeed according to any virtue or merit that belongs to our application [of Christ's satisfaction to us]—not, in other words, according to any merit that belongs to our faith—but according to the virtue and merit of Christ's cross and satisfaction. Nevertheless God will not fulfil unto us that promise in the covenant without faith on our part. Therefore the proper and peculiar condition of the covenant of grace consists in Christ's satisfaction, which is the efficient and meritorious cause of the fulfilling of the promise, and in our faith, as in a kind of subservient and instrumental cause. We see from this also that the condition of the new covenant is itself the same as that cause [*causa*] which first moved God to renew the covenant, and to settle this covenant of grace with man. I understand that cause to be Christ the mediator and his own satisfaction. But by a certain reckoning we consider the condition of the covenant to be something other than that cause.

Indeed, Christ's satisfaction, as something already completed in the past, moved God to renew the covenant. The same satisfaction is the condition of the covenant, but that as something which is, as it were, in the future—not of course in relation to Christ, but in relation to us—insofar as that very satisfaction must without any doubt be apprehended by us, in order that the promise of the covenant might be fulfilled to us. For the promise in any covenant follows, properly speaking, upon something to be fulfilled in the future [relative to the promise *per se*]; so the condition in the covenant of works was works which we were yet to perform. In light, therefore, of what we have said about the condition of the gratuitous covenant, it is surely apparent that this covenant is founded entirely upon the grace of God, and this not only with respect to that cause—namely, the satisfaction of the mediator—which moved God to establish it, but also with respect to the condition of the covenant, which flows entirely from the grace of God, and in no way our own virtues. For Christ's satisfaction is of grace, and our faith is a pure gift from God. Therefore the condition of the gratuitous covenant, whether you have regard to Christ crucified or our faith, is far from anything that might detract from the grace of God; indeed with a view towards these very things—namely, Christ's satisfaction and our faith—we must say that the condition of this covenant is rooted in the grace of God.

But you might say: Since Christ, by his satisfaction, both merited the covenant itself and procured the fulfilment of the covenant and promise, how can it be called gratuitous? I respond: It is not called gratuitous with regard to Christ's part in it, since he merited both the covenant itself and the fulfilment of the covenant, but with regard to our part in it. For that satisfaction and that merit are not ours, except through faith. Nor can we speak of "merit" when we look to our part in the covenant, but only of "grace," both because Christ has been given unto us as a mediator by the grace of God, and because God, as a result of his own grace, accepts that satisfaction of Christ's, apprehended by our faith, as if it were our own. This covenant was established immediately after the fall of man. From that time forward it has been repeated, albeit rather obscurely under the law and, in truth, more openly under grace. This covenant of grace can indeed be comprehended in several words; that is, in the promise of justice and life held forth under the condition of faith. But God, in consideration of our faith, willed this covenant of grace to be declared and explained more extensively in his gospel, just as the covenant of works was explicated in the doctrine of the law.

And so in the gospel, and primarily in the New Testament (as it is called), we learn about Jesus Christ the mediator, about his humiliation and his glorification, and finally about the benefits promised in the covenant—remission of sins, justification, sanctification, and eternal life. And so the gospel which we hold in our hands, and the whole preaching of that gospel, is nothing other than the doctrine of God's gratuitous covenant declared and explained more extensively and fully. And so Paul, in Rom 10, summarizes that word of faith, that is, the gospel, in these words: "If you confess with your mouth the Lord Jesus, and believe in your heart that God has raised him from the dead, you will be saved." From this it is apparent that the entire doctrine of the gospel is reducible to this covenant and the promise which it contains; and thus the gospel is nothing other than a fuller explication of the covenant. But if someone cuts himself off from this covenant of grace, no further sacrifice remains for that man; indeed, this would be to demand a new mediator (Heb 6:6 & 10:26).

To this gratuitous covenant of God, and its proclamation in the gospel, a sacrament has been added, on account of the infirmity and weakness of our faith. The end and use of the sacrament is twofold: first, to represent by a certain sign, more so than the word of the covenant and the gospel by itself could, those very spiritual realities which were previously indicated and announced by the word, and to represent also the inward application of those precious realities, and so indeed to apply, as a kind of instrument, those very realities. From this first end and use the second and principal end follows, which is to confirm unto us the word; that is, to work in us, so that we believe more strongly that word of the covenant and gospel. Thus, I say, the latter end of the sacrament is confirmation of the word of the covenant and gospel. I do not mean that the sacrament ratifies or makes certain the covenant in and of itself, or with respect to God and his making of the covenant with man (because this sacrament could not be greater than the sacrifice of the mediator). I mean, rather, that the sacrament makes that covenant of God more certain to us, in light of our weakness and the quality of our faith. By means of its visible representation of the mediator's cross, his benefits, and the interior application of those benefits, which things the word has communicated already in the covenant, the sacrament works to make us believe more strongly in the word of that covenant. It is clear, from this latter end of the sacrament, that the word itself of the covenant and the gospel is prior and superior to the sacrament. For an end is always prior and superior to whatever thing is destined towards that end. And so the word, taken on its own, if compared to the sacrament on its own, is better than the sacrament. But if the sacrament is added to the word, then it becomes more excellent, more powerful, and ultimately more effective than the word alone for the confirmation of our faith.

But let us return to the first use of the sacrament, and say something more about it. The sacrament exhibits before our eyes Christ the mediator crucified and his benefits. It does not exhibit these things as naked realities having no bearing upon us, but rather, in truth, with a view towards their inward application to us. And it proves to be an effective instrument of the Holy Spirit for the accomplishing of that inward application. The exhibition and application of these things do not belong first and foremost to the sacrament, but to the word. For the word of the covenant and the gospel first signifies and applies these spiritual realities, and so is a kind of audible sign of them. Then, on account of our infirmity, the sacrament represents and applies these things to us to a greater extent, by placing them as living realities, as it were, before our eyes, and offering them to us to be handled with our own hands. And thus the sacrament sends us back to the word, as to the principal sign and organ of the Spirit, and works to make us believe more strongly in that word, which is the latter and principal end of the sacrament, an end commonly referred to as the confirmation and sealing of the covenant (concerning which, see Rom 4:11).

Now the causes of this first use of the sacrament ought to be considered. We should consider, first of all, the reasons [*causae*] that those spiritual realities which are first announced in the word can be represented and applied in the sacrament. Then we should ask why the sacrament can represent and apply these things better than the word by itself can. There are, then, two causes, quite simply, for the sacrament's representation and application of these spiritual realities. The first is the analogy and symmetry between the sign and thing signified. So in baptism there is some symmetry between water and the blood of Christ. In the supper of the Lord there is some symmetry between the bread and Christ's body, and between the wine and Christ's blood.

The same judgment applies to the rituals involved in each sacrament, which are also signs, and have their own likeness and symmetry to the internal realities and actions [which they represent and apply]. This analogy or proportion arises from a natural quality existing in the sign, by virtue of which the sign is similar to the thing signified. So, for example, there is a natural property in the water used in baptism to make one clean; this being so, the water is similar to the blood of the Lord. And in the supper of the

Lord there is a natural property in the bread to feed and nourish a man; this being so, the bread is similar to the body of Christ. For indeed, unless some analogy or proportion existed between a sign and whatever thing it signified, that sign could not reasonably be a sign of the thing signified. So, for example, grass cannot be a sign of man, since there is no analogy or proportion between that proposed sign and the thing signified.

A second cause of the sacrament's representation and application of spiritual realities is that union between sacrament and spiritual realities which is called "sacramental." This union consists in a mutual relationship of sign and thing signified, which relationship existing, the sign is no sooner set before the eyes than the thing signified is set before the soul and the eyes of faith. For there is a special character between the things related, such that no sooner is one recognized than the other springs to the mind. And so I say that in order for this representation and application to exist, and thus the sacrament as such, there must be a sacramental union between sign and thing signified. Neither, indeed, is it sufficient to make a sacrament that some representation and application of spiritual things exists by mere similitude and proportion; for then all bread, all wine, and all water would be sacraments, since there exists a certain similitude between all bread, all wine, and all water, and the body and blood of our Lord.

Moreover, this relation that I am describing springs not from the nature of that very thing which is the sign; for example, from the nature of the water in baptism, or of the bread and wine in the Lord's Supper, etc. Rather this relation descends supernaturally to the signs in the sacrament, and proceeds from the institution of God and of Christ. So, for example, in baptism, the water does not have something within its own nature to make it a sign or sacrament of the blood of the Lord; for then, again, all water would be a sacrament and would have this relation to the blood of the Lord. Rather, it has this relation to, and is a sacrament of, Christ's blood by virtue of the institution and ordination of the Lord himself, according to which that water is transferred from common to sacred use, and becomes a sacrament of the Lord's blood. This same judgment applies to the signs in the sacrament of the Supper.

Moreover, this institution or "consecration," as it is called, exists through prayer and the word by which the use of those external things is explained; for example, the use of that water in baptism, and of that bread and wine in the Lord's Supper. Thus it is said in the Supper "this is my body." In other words, "this bread is a sign or sacrament of my body, and has now the use of representing my body." The one who institutes and consecrates the sacrament—that is, the architect of the sacrament, the one who makes the sacrament as such, and clearly transforms an element from common to sacred use (a transformation that cannot come from a creature)—is properly speaking the Lord himself. This he did first of all *per se* in the last supper; now, however, he does this through men, not indeed all men without distinction, but those legitimately called; that is, his pastors and ministers. Where this does not happen through his pastors and ministers, the sacrament is not a sacrament, but a desecration of the same. Such are the causes of that representation and application of simple heavenly realities which occurs through the sacrament. The reason, moreover, that the sacrament can better represent and apply these heavenly realities than the word by itself is that the word only offers these things to our hearing, while the sacrament represents them also to other senses, particularly our vision and touch, so that these heavenly realities can be seen (as it were) by our eyes, and handled with our hands.

Thus far concerning the ends of the sacrament, especially that first end. Now something should be said about the signs in the sacrament, and about the right division of them. I call "signs" not only the elements themselves, but also the rituals and external actions related to the elements in the sacrament: in baptism, the pouring of water, and washing with water; in the Lord's Supper, the breaking of bread, the pouring of wine, the distribution of bread and wine, the reception of bread and wine, and the eating and drinking of bread and wine. I name the things signified as Christ (who is both man and God), his cross, and his benefits. These things, moreover, are signified in the sacrament first of all simply and absolutely, and

On the Sacrament

then with a view towards their application to us. From this reality springs the division of signs: for we identify some of the signs as signs of spiritual things themselves *per se*; others we identify, in truth, as signs of the application of those spiritual things. Those things which I call signs of spiritual things themselves *per se* represent and signify those spiritual realities more so than the word by itself. These things are also, I confess, instruments and organs of the Holy Spirit, by which our minds are more greatly illumined, and through which increases that first part of faith, our knowledge, which has already taken root by the proclamation of the word.

This category of signs can be made clearer by application of our teaching to the specific sacraments. In baptism, first of all, the signs of spiritual realities themselves *per se* are the following: water, which is a sign of Christ's blood and of his substance; the pouring of water, which is a sign of Christ's cross and passion, and also of all the benefits which flow from his passion. Here it should be noted that whatever is the sign of Christ's passion in each sacrament is also the sign, in my judgment, of those benefits which flow from his cross and passion. Next, with regard to the Lord's Supper, the sign of those heavenly realities themselves *per se* are the following: bread, which is a sign of the body and substance of Christ; wine, which is a sign of Christ's blood and, again, his substance; the breaking of bread, which is a sign of the crucifixion of his body, and also of the benefits which flow from his cross; the pouring of wine, which is a sign of the effusion of his blood on the cross, and also of the benefits which flow from that effusion.

Thus far concerning the signs of spiritual realities themselves *per se*. I name as signs of the application of those same things—namely, Christ's substance, his cross, and finally his benefits—those rituals which not only represent [the application of these realities] more than the word [by itself] and serve as instruments for our cognition of the internal application of those spiritual realities, but are in truth also effective instruments of the Holy Spirit for the increase, in our hearts, of that very internal application which they represent so well. Therefore these signs pertain to the increase of that second part of our faith, which we say consists in the heart's apprehension [of Christ, his cross, and his benefits], just as those prior signs, which we have called signs of spiritual realities themselves *per se*, pertain to that first part of faith, and to the increase of that which belongs to knowledge. So it is that while those former signs [of spiritual realities *per se*] can be said to represent spiritual realities, these latter signs can be properly said to apply spiritual realities. This, moreover, is why the sacraments are called especially signs and seals (*sphragides*).

This latter category of signs we will illustrate with examples from each sacrament. In baptism, the sign of application is washing, which is undoubtedly a sign, first of all, of the application of Christ's blood and substance to us, and secondly of the application of his cross to us, and thirdly of the application of all the benefits which flow from his cross to us. For this should at once be noted concerning the signs of application in each sacrament, that each one is a sign of the application of all those realities—Christ's substance, his cross, and his benefits—simultaneously. In the Lord's Supper there are four signs of application: the distribution of elements both on the part of Christ and his ministers; the reception of elements on the part of the people and by each and every individual among the people; the eating of bread and then drinking of wine on the part of the people and by each and every individual among the people. These singular signs constitute the signs of the application of all those heavenly realities: Christ, his cross, and his benefits.

Now if you compare the two kinds of signs we have noted, you will see from the definition of each kind that those which we have called signs of application exceed by one grade, and by that are distinguished from, those signs which we have called signs of heavenly realities *per se*. For while there are two realities at work in the signs *per se*—first, that they represent those spiritual realities, and so are signs as such; and second, that they open the eyes of our minds, and so are instruments of the Holy Spirit to make us see internal spiritual realities in these external signs of things (for unless these signs were instruments also of the Spirit to open our eyes, they could never in fact be signs to us of those things)—while, I say, there are two realities at work in the signs of these realities themselves *per se*, there are three realities at work in the signs of application: first, they represent to us the internal application of those spiritual realities; second, they are organs of the Holy Spirit for opening the eyes of our minds, so that we should see, as it were, in those external signs the application of those internal, spiritual realities; and third, they are instruments of the Holy Spirit for effecting in our hearts the application of those same, internal, heavenly realities. And in this third function, as it were, these signs of application exceed, in degree of excellence, that other, prior category of signs which we have called signs of realities themselves *per se*.

Thus far concerning the division of signs in the sacrament. Now, finally, from these things which we have said about the sacrament in general, some general definition of "sacrament" ought to be deduced: therefore, we define a sacrament as a visible sign instituted by God by which, on one hand, these heavenly realities are represented more so than they are signified by the word itself, and on the other hand, the same realities are truly and to a greater extent applied to us; and this [the sacrament accomplishes] both on account of a certain analogy and a sacramental union [between sign and thing signified], and also on account of the visibility, as indeed I have said, of the signs. From this, in turn, it happens that the sacrament confirms our faith in the word of the covenant and gospel, and it effects in us greater faith in the same. In this definition "sign" functions as *genus*; the first distinction, then, of a sacrament [in relation to signs more generally] follows from the institution of God, by which the sacrament is set apart from all other profane and common signs. A second distinction of the sacrament consists in the fact that it is a visible sign, which sets it apart from the word which is a kind of audible sign instituted by God. A third distinction of the sacrament is assumed in that first use of the sacrament defined above, which is that it represents and applies certain heavenly realities more than the word by itself can do. And in this again the sacrament is distinguished from the word of God, which also signifies and applies those heavenly realities; the distinction, however, lies in the fact that the sacrament, annexed to the word, signifies and applies the same realities to a greater extent than the word by itself can do. These distinctions, with regard to the definition of the sacrament, are all subsumed into that first use of the sacrament and its causes, about which we have spoken above. A fourth distinction of the sacrament follows from and consists in that latter and principal use of the sacrament, which use has been described as the confirmation to us of that word of the covenant and gospel, and the working in us to believe that word more strongly, in much the same way that a seal added to a diplomatic letter confirms that letter and encourages greater confidence in it. This latter use of the sacrament follows from the former. For since the sacrament signifies and applies to us to a greater extent those same realities which are previously signified and applied by the word, how can it not at the same time confirm the word about those things, and produce greater faith in that word?

From all these things that have been said about the sacrament it is apparent that, if we wish to employ properly the word "sacrament," we must not allow any confusion whatsoever between the [sacramental] sign and the thing signified; indeed, the external sign must be distinguished from, yet held in relation to, that thing which it signifies. For the relation [of sign and thing signified] is such that these things, which are said to be correlated, are not confounded; in truth, this relation declares the nature of each thing related to the other. For the nature of the relation is such that each reality [i.e., sign and thing signified] exists in proper relation to, and respect of, the other.

To summarize what has been said about the sacrament in general: first we have spoken about the covenant which is the foundation of the sacrament; then we have spoken about the sacrament itself—the twofold use of the sacrament, the signs of the sacrament, and, finally, the definition of the sacrament. From all these things which have been said about the sacrament in general, the nature of each particular sacrament can be easily determined. So we can see that baptism is nothing other than a sacrament by which the covenant of grace, already established, is confirmed.

And so we can see that the Lord's Supper is nothing other than a sacrament by which the same covenant of grace is confirmed, and that, to be sure, over an extended period of time; or we might say, to put it another way, that the Supper is a sacrament by which one's progress in the covenant of grace—progress being discerned in the increase of faith—is confirmed. This definition of each particular sacrament has been obtained from a special consideration of the latter use of the sacrament.

On Good Works[1]

From our discussion of justification and glorification, there follows a question about good works, which are effects of glorification. Concerning them it is customary to ask whether or not they might justify a man. A good work, or a work pleasing to God, is one which conforms to his own law and will. The law of God requires, in whatever deed is done, not merely the outward appearance of a good deed, but also inward sincerity of the heart. For, then, a work to be good and to conform to the divine law, it must not only be done—so far as the substance of the work goes—according to God's command, but must also, in truth, be done in the manner which God has instructed. That is, there must be a sincere heart, as a kind of fountain of external actions, as well as consideration for the glory of God himself, as the peculiar end for which a work is performed, which consideration for God's glory necessarily follows from a sincere heart. In a good work, therefore, there are these three ingredients: first, conformity to God's law; second, inward sincerity of the heart; and third, consideration for God's glory, flowing from that sincerity.

With regard to these three things, it is apparent that the principle and form of a good work—that which a work possesses that permits it to be called "good"—is, so to speak, ἐινομίαν or conformity to the law. And the principle and form of sin, or of an evil work, is a certain ἀνομία and diversion from the law. Prior

---

1. Excerpted from Rollock, *Epistolam ad Romanos*, 202–18.

to the fall, man, being at that time sincere in heart, was disposed by his very nature unto good works. But now, after the fall, that sincerity of heart—and, indeed, uprightness in every faculty of the soul—has been lost, and man, having become a fool, entirely avoids good works. It can, of course, happen that an unregenerate man brings forth some deed which possesses external conformity to the revealed will of God, as when he does not kill, does not commit adultery, does not steal, and so on. But because, in truth, the divine law specifically demands that fountain of sincerity in the heart, and flowing from that regard unto divine glory, the work of an unregenerate man—no matter how attractive—cannot simply and properly be called a "good work." Indeed, such work is not living, but—as the Apostle names it—dead and hypocritical.[2]

Man already regenerated, having through faith recovered some portion of sincerity of heart, can by virtue of that portion be described as ready unto good works—according to that measure, of course, in which integrity and sincerity of heart has been recuperated. But the work of a regenerate man is good only according to its share of conformity to the law, and does not give all that is required to the law of God, who is most holy and most perfect. Hence it does not, insofar as it possesses even the smallest degree of imperfection, satisfy God. For, then, a work to be satisfying to God and to conform to his own law and will, it must appear, as it were, before him—it must be led into his own light and view—cloaked in Christ's merit, which is apprehended by faith. Thus it is said in Rom 14:23, "whatever does not proceed from faith is sin." And similarly in Heb 11:6, "without faith it is impossible to please him," which statement means not only that man's heart, by faith in Jesus Christ, is made clean and recovers some part of its sincerity and integrity, but also, in truth, that the imperfection of works proceeding from a heart only in part reborn are covered by that same faith. Therefore faith accomplishes two things with regard to the good work of the regenerate man: first, it purifies the heart and fount of that good work (Acts 15:9); and second, it covers, as it were, the defects of that work which proceeds from a heart only

---

2. Cf. Heb 6:1 and 9:14.

partially reborn. The work of the man without faith, moreover, suffers a twofold loss: first, without faith there is clearly no beginning of regeneration, from whence that work should proceed; and second, without faith there is no veil for the impurity under which that work labors.

The things said so far about the good works of man are seen, first of all, in man's state of innocence before the fall, secondly in the state of corruption after the fall, and thirdly in the state of regeneration. Now let us consider whether works have merit in this threefold state of man. Merit, indeed, is something which is consequent and bound to a work, and looks either to a reward for well-doing, or to punishment for evil-doing. Merit leading to punishment is usually referred to as "guilt" for sin. Merit leading to reward typically retains the name "merit." Merit in general looks to some compensation or ἀντιμισθίαν (Rom 1:27). Now this compensation is either one of punishment or one of reward. And compensation for that which is generally referred to as merit is also called μισθός or "wages." The word "wages" is likewise general, for "wages" can either be reward or punishment. Debt is related to wages in the general sense of the term "wages," just as merit is to work. For "wages" are properly nothing other than that which is given according to debt. Indeed, the giving of something [in consequence of some debt] is a general reality, but we ultimately distinguish the giving of something as either "grace" or "debt," depending on which of those two realities—grace or debt—gives rise to the giving. For something given is either given of grace, and so is a free gift, or of debt, and so is wages—although the word "wages" is a generic term, and is sometimes used to refer more generally to things that are given, whether those things be given of grace or of debt. Thus Rom 4:4 says: "To the one who works, wages are reckoned not of grace, but of debt."

From this it follows that wages might also be reckoned according to grace, and so the word "wages" can signify a free gift. In Luke 6:32, that which is given to man is called χάρις—that is, "grace," or a free gift—while in Matthew 6:1, that which is given to man is called μισθός—that is, "wages," or something delivered according to debt. Therefore the word "wages" is ambiguous, and is adjusted to the particular species of something being given or reckoned. Now if, surely, the rule of debt—that which establishes "wages" properly called—is sought, it will appear that debt properly exists where someone is obligated to give something to another according to the order of justice, because of the worth of benefits previously received from that other. Indeed, merit—or a meritorious work—is properly one to which recompense is owed, according to the order of justice, on account of the worth of that work—and the recompense that is owed is called "wages." And from these things which we have said, we have the proper meaning of "debt." But improperly, "debt" signifies something that is owed not according to the order of justice—and thus not, surely, according to any obligation arising from the value of benefits received—but according to a covenant and gratuitous promise; that is, not because the worth of a work or benefit received requires something in return, but because there is an agreement or covenant to give something in return for the work. Similarly, "merit"—or "meritorious work"—can be improperly applied to a deed which requires a reward and retribution not, indeed, according to the order of justice, on account of the worth of the deed, but according to a covenant, even though there be no parity whatsoever between the deed done and the reward (Rom 8:18).

These things being established, we say that an evil deed is meritorious according to the proper meaning of the word "merit," and that punishment is due an evil deed according to the proper meaning of "debt." For wages are rendered to an evil deed on account of the very worth of that deed, according to the order of justice. But if we are talking about a good work, we deny that any good work, even the most extraordinary, of a creature merits anything—if we accept the word "merit" according to its simple meaning—from God. We deny that God owes anything to a good work, if we accept the words "debt" and "wages" properly. For no good work whatsoever has enough worth to compel God to distribute wages to it according to the order of justice. I do not, however, entirely deny, in discussing a good work, that it merits something from God according to some covenant and the gratuitous promise of God himself, and that, similarly, something is owed to that work according to the covenant and gratuitous promise. But I would willingly abstain from these expressions regarding merit and debt, from which expressions sacred Scripture itself shrinks back, speaking throughout of nothing other than pure grace. And God's grace is conspicuous in this, that he not only considers work (and that imperfect) that we ourselves owe to him—owe, I say, on account of infinite benefits already bestowed upon us in the past—pleasing and acceptable, but in a certain way even compensates such work with that greatest of benefits, eternal life. However much, therefore, is attributed to merit, so much is detracted from God's grace. And as often as the notion of some merit of our own, once conceived in the mind, flourishes (as it were) in our hearts, let it be entirely uprooted by the preaching of grace. And grace is especially discerned in this, that it rewards works which are not meritorious, but rather owed to God, with even the greatest of God's benefits. To be sure, Scripture uses the word "wages" to name God's gratuitous gift to one who is said to do good works, but in doing so the word is always received in a less than proper manner of speaking. So Scripture does not support the Papists' dream about a constant relationship between wages and merit—as if, in truth, "wages" always indicate something which is owed, whether simply or according to a covenant.

Thus far we have dealt with the words "merit," "wages," and "debt." Now let us pursue the application of that which has been proposed concerning merit to works in that threefold condition of man. In the state of innocence the works of man should have been perfect, and should have answered entirely to God's law. Therefore we should not deny that God would have recompensed those works with his reward, and this according to debt—not, indeed, debt *per se*, but according to his own pact and gratuitous promise which was made in the covenant of works. I say according to debt not *per se* but in keeping with his covenant because no creature, no matter how perfect, possesses merit before his Creator. "For who has given to God, that God should repay him?" Rom 11:35.

On Good Works

And "what creature has anything that he has not received." 1 Cor 4:7. So the work of a creature, no matter how perfect, is properly and simply duty—something which the creature is obliged to do; something which is, indeed, a mere trifling if measured against God the Creator and his immeasurable benefits to the creature. The work of a creature is, I say, duty; it is no merit. Hence Luke 17:10 reads, "When you have done all that you were commanded, say, 'We are unworthy servants; we have only done what was our duty.'" It should be noted that Scripture does, in truth, speak about wages owed to works, and those perfect. "To the one," Rom 4:4 says, "who works, his wages are reckoned according to debt." However, we find in Scripture no word about the merit of works, even those that are most perfect. Indeed, Scripture contains no word meaning "merit" in those passages, Ecclesiasticus 16:15 and Hebrews 13:16, where the ancient translator [Jerome] mentioned merit, though perhaps it speaks of some debt of God which is in accordance with his own liberality and grace rather than the true and proper rule of merit, which assigns wages to work done that was not owed according to the order of justice.

Thus far concerning the merit of good works in the state of innocence. In the state of corruption before regeneration, I confess that there is, in truth, no debt, or merit, or reward—that is, no debt or merit of life—even according to a covenant, unless you speak of the debt or merit of punishment and eternal death. "For the wages of sin is death." Rom 6:23. Indeed, works of those who are not regenerate, even if they might sometimes possess some outward conformity to the law of God, should not—at least with regard to the one who performs them—be called good, because they do not proceed from a sincere heart, nor do they proceed from faith. "For whatever is not of faith, is sin." Rom 14:23. And again, "without faith it is impossible to please God." Heb 11:6. Nevertheless, there are different degrees of evil works, and not all sins are equal. Those are much worse, to be sure, that conform not at all, not even outwardly, to the law of God—for example, adultery, murder, etc., which acts are most clearly contrary to God's law. Works which outwardly conform to God's law are not evil to such a degree, but they are evil, for without that inward sincerity of heart they are necessarily hypocritical.

Moving on from these things, we come now to speak about the merit of good works in the state of regeneration, which is where the entire controversy lies. And we assert that the works of regenerate man are no merits. Nor is anything owed to such works by God, even according to a covenant and promise. And the principle reason for this is that we are not now living under that covenant of works that God enters into with man, the covenant made with a condition of works of the law. We are, rather, under the covenant of grace that God enters into with man, and so under the condition of Christ's merit to be apprehended by our faith, not under the condition of works. Those, therefore, who defend the merit of regenerate man's works, and God's debt to the same—even insofar as they say this debt is not such simply but according to the covenant, which point we might allow them—do nothing, I say, but confine us once again under the covenant of works, and drive us back into slavery to the law, from which we have been freed through Christ. But there is a further reason that God owes nothing to the works of regenerate man. For even if we were to grant that we are still under the covenant of works, and that God should weigh our works according to the terms of that covenant, we nevertheless say that God would owe nothing to our works, and we would merit nothing from God according to the promise made in that covenant, unless you intend death. For our works, even in the state of regeneration, are imperfect, and will not measure up to the rule of God's law, unless perhaps you make that most holy and perfect law of God a lesbian rule (such as the present-day Papists do).

Our adversaries oppose these arguments which we have drawn together. With regard, first of all, to that principal reason we have indicated that God does not owe anything to regenerate man's works, they say: "Is it not the case that even throughout the New Testament many benefits—both temporary and eternal—are promised to us for our good works? As 1 Tim 4:8 says, 'Godliness is most useful, holding forth promise for both this life and the next.' If, then, Scripture promises good, even in the gospel, under the condition of our works, it clearly follows that we are not freed from that covenant of works, and that God even now owes something to us for our works, at least according to his covenant."

I answer with a distinction regarding the antecedent in this argument. To say that God, in the gospel, promises good things under the condition of works, which works themselves should procure unto us those promised goods, is false. To say that good works demonstrate and prove, as notable effects in us, that we are sharers in that condition comprised in the covenant of grace, and which alone, being fulfilled, is able to procure those goods, is true. When this distinction has been made with regard to the antecedent, we see that it does not follow that we are under the covenant of works, so that, even according to the covenant, something should be owed to our good works. So if a promise was set forth under the condition of works, it was not done to the end that we should procure the promised goods by our works themselves. This should be clear, first of all, from the imperfection of our works, which is something that we not only feel ourselves but Scripture confirms. It should be clear, moreover, from the testimonies of Scripture which show that works are required in the gospel for no other end than this, that we might live consistently with the gospel, that is, the new covenant and our calling. See Eph 4:1.

But this whole matter might be avoided if we make a distinction between, on one hand, the promises in the gospel which are made under the condition of works and, on the other, the promises and covenants of the law. For those promises which occur within the New Testament under the condition of works, are, in the first place, all made in Christ and because of Christ and his merit. And, in the next place, those promises which are made because of Christ and his merit are fulfilled because of Christ alone and his merit. Thus the compensation or reward which is rendered to our works is not done so because the condition of works has been fulfilled, and this according to his covenant, so that God has now become a debtor to us. For those very works of regeneration are so imperfect that unless they should obtain favor in Christ they would procure certain damnation. And, thirdly, we say that those promises which have some condition of works in the gospel are not made by God to that end that we should be justified or saved through our works—that is, that we should acquire for ourselves those promised benefits according to our works. Rather, those promises are made to the end that we should be stirred up unto a life which is worthy of Christ, in whom alone we obtain all things, and his gospel. "I beseech you," says Eph 4:1, "to walk in a manner worthy of that calling with which you have been called."

With respect to that covenant of works, moreover, we note, first, that it was not made on account of Christ the mediator. Secondly, that the promise in the covenant of works, if man had remained upright, would not have been fulfilled because of Christ, but because of that fulfilled condition of works. And finally, that the covenant of works was made to the end that we might procure for ourselves, according to God's covenant, the wages promised and fulfilled by him. From these considerations it follows that those promises which occur in the gospel, which are made under some condition of good works, pertain not at all to the law and the covenant of works. For the covenant of works can in no way stand together with Christ and the covenant of grace in him. Neither does the covenant of works retain any use with regard to us who are now under the covenant of grace and the gospel, except this, that being compelled to terror and dismay by it we might seek Christ and that covenant of grace which is established in him. And the covenant of works had this particular use also in relation to God's people of old. Thus in Deut 18, God actually commends the people for professing, with these words, their own dismay at that audible voice of Jehovah promulgating his own law. In vs. 16 we read: "Let me not hear again that voice of Jehovah God, neither let me see anymore that great fire, lest I die." And God commends, in vs. 17, this statement with these words: "Therefore Jehovah said to me, 'The words which they have spoken have been spoken well.'" And then, in vs. 18, God made a promise of Christ the mediator, to whom he evidently wished the people to flee, leaving behind them the law and the covenant of works: "I will raise up for them

On Good Works

from among their own brothers a prophet like you, and I will put my words in his mouth, and he shall speak to them all that I will command him." Paul, writing to the Galatians, nods to this use of the law and the covenant of works when he says that the law was a pedagogue leading us to Christ, in order that we might be justified by faith. Moreover, the apostle writing to the Hebrews clearly indicates that we who are in Christ have been freed from that covenant and from the terrors of the law (Heb 12:18). In sum, the gospel is full of such sentiments; see for example Romans 6–8.

We have determined to say nothing substantial at this time, and in this short work, about those objections that are brought against that second reason we have produced that regenerate man's works merit nothing from God—that is, the imperfection of our good works—because such objections have already been answered more than a thousand times by pious and learned men. We will at this time merely lay hold of several words that are used to buttress the merit of good works, and will respond to the same in several words.

"Is it not the case," our adversaries say in the first place, "that the works of regenerate men please God?" I answer that both the regenerate persons themselves and their works please God. We see in Heb 11:5 that the person of Enoch pleased God. Therefore his works did also. In addition, I say that God not only considers the works of regenerate men pleasing, but he also follows them, and as it were compensates them, with both spiritual and temporal blessings. But it does not follow from this that works are meritorious. Works, indeed, are neither pleasing to God nor compensated by him because they themselves merit anything from God, even according to a covenant. In truth, they possess that which pleases God only from Christ's merit apprehended by faith. It was in this way that Enoch is said to have been pleasing to God (Heb 11:5–6). For by the merit of Christ, in the first place, the wrath of God, which is earned by the imperfection of even the holiest of men's works, is turned aside. And by that same merit, in the next place, grace is acquired for our imperfect works. "Therefore," you say, "Christ's merit is, in all events, distributed to men in order that they might then merit God's favor and grace." I answer that this is poorly reasoned. For it is not the case that Christ died for us in order to merit for us some merit for ourselves and our own works. I admit that he merited for us multitudinous grace—justification, regeneration, and finally eternal life. However, he has not merited our right or ability to merit for ourselves even the least benefit, much less so those peculiar benefits of justification and eternal life. For it would necessarily detract both from Christ's own merit and the grace of God in his Son if we should have come to share merit with Christ, and not have been fixed upon the merit of Christ alone. Most ungodly, therefore, is that evasion of the Papists, who actually wish to appear most modest in this business about the merit of works when they say that Christ's merit gives power and efficacy to our own meritorious works. For what is this but to establish the merit of our works also, even if it be conceded that such merit truly results from the power of Christ's merit? More honest was Paul, who saying first of all in Rom 4:4 that "to the one who works wages are not reckoned according to grace," so distinguished works and grace that to establish works would be to deny grace. And again in Rom 11:6 he established disagreement between those works which men call meritorious and grace—for when one of these is established, the other is declared to be immediately and necessarily destroyed. The same thing should be declared about Christ's merit and our own meritorious works. For Christ's merit and grace stand together. Thus, the merit of our own works being once established—however and wherever this is done, whether our own merit be primary or secondary—Christ's merit is already destroyed. Conversely, Christ's merit being established, any merit whatsoever of man is already completely destroyed.

Now, finally, we must say something about the final judgment more broadly, because the pattern of that future and final judgment is thought to be established according to the merit of one's own works. Scripture expresses in a few words the rule and pattern of the future judgment: "God will render to every man according to his works" (Psa 61:12; Matt 16:27; Rom 2:6; Rev 22:12). You have a description of this sentence and of the formula for the divine judgment in Matt 25:34ff., Rom 2:7ff., 2 Thess 1:6ff., and other places. Therefore, God's sentence in that future judgment will be brought forward according to works; that is, God will make his judgment according to works. As, at that time, works which have been done in life, whether good or evil, are found, so will God bring forward his sentence, whether of life or death. Since, then, there is no controversy about that sentence being brought about according to our works, it is asked: "Are not those works, according to which sentence will be made, causes for the procuring and meriting of that compensation, whether of life or death?" I respond thus: if we are speaking about the works of reprobate men, I certainly do not deny that they are the cause of that future sentence of death which shall be applied to them. But the whole question is about the works of the elect. Will God also pronounce his sentence of life in the last judgment according to works as a meritorious cause? Concerning this, then, I affirm that God will declare his sentence of eternal life according to the works of the elect, and will compensate his elect according to their works, not indeed as causes of that life or compensation, but as certain effects which provide testimony to the causes themselves. The causes, however, are the decree of God from eternity, and our calling and justification in time. These are proven to be the true and unique causes by that singular text in Matthew 25, in which we have the express pattern of the future judgment. "Come," the text says, "you who are blessed of my Father, and inherit the kingdom of my Father which has been prepared for you from before the foundation of the world." This manner of speaking to the elect and discharging of them into the kingdom of heaven sufficiently proves that the cause of the elect's being sent to possess the kingdom of heaven lies outside of themselves, and is found in the gratuitous blessing of God through Christ. "You are blessed," it says, "of my Father." For blessing does not come to us through merit, but through grace in Christ, "who has freed us from the curse of the law to which we are by nature liable, having been made a curse for us" (Gal 3:14). And "the Father has blessed us with every spiritual blessing in Christ." Eph 1:3. Blessing in Christ, then, contains within itself our calling and justification. Indeed, these are the parts of God's blessing in time. The words of Matthew 25 further prove that the cause of our salvation rests in God's eternal decree, according to which the kingdom that the elect are being sent to possess has been prepared for them.

But you might object that these causes which are outside of us, of which mention has just been made, in no way prevent our good works from also being causes of our future life, since even in the same chapter of Matthew, verse 41, the causes for that death to which the reprobate are assigned are identified as God's cursing and God's decree. "You who are cursed," the verse says, "depart from me into eternal fire," etc. But these causes do not impede at all the very works of reprobate men from also being causes of their condemnation in the future judgment. "Thus," you say, "by the same logic, the good works of the elect are causes of their salvation, besides those causes already mentioned." I will grant our adversaries their antecedent—to some extent the reason for the reprobate's condemnation and ruin lies in God's decree—but what they argue by the force of similarity does not follow. I have shown that there is no parity between the reckoning of evil works and that of good works. (For evil works are perfectly evil, and that which is so plainly evil merits death, while good works are imperfectly good, and only that which is pure and perfect in all its parts could procure life, even according to a covenant.) I have, I say, shown this—unless it now should become clearer even by its own light. I only add now that occasionally in Scripture the cause of judgment and of life is manifestly reckoned as faith. So in 2 Thess 1:10 it says, "When he comes to be glorified in his saints, and to be marveled at by all the faithful (because our testimony to you was received in faith) on that day." From these words it is clear that the glorification of God in the salvation of the faithful on that day will be from this: that the gospel was believed. Therefore the salvation of the saints, and the glory of God according to their salvation, will be on account of faith.

But in this matter I stick to what I have said, since Paul's discussion of justification by faith and that alone sufficiently shows that the justification of man, or the sentence of justice and life, is not indeed according to works as causes of the same, but rather by faith alone, whether you should consider this present life or that which is future. "But," you will say, "in these words 'Come you who are blessed, etc.,' there is only an address and judicial judgment unto life. In what follows we see the cause for that judgment: 'For I was hungry and you gave me food, etc.'" I respond that this reason given for entering into life is not an *a priori* one, or a cause, but an *a posteriori* one, or effects which demonstrate both that the kingdom has been prepared from eternity and that faith has appeared in time—that is, effects which provide testimony that believers have been predestined unto life from eternity, and have been called and justified in time. For this is the sense of what is said: "By your good works you have provided witness to your election and to those mediate causes which hinge upon the same, your calling and justification." Or to state this more clearly, the sense of what is said is this: "Enter into heaven, because you are blessed and have been destined for the heavenly kingdom. For you—persons of holy lives—have shown yourselves by your good works to be blessed, that is, called and justified in time, and thenceforth destined from eternity to the heavenly kingdom, which is the reason that I bid you enter into heaven." Indeed, the cause of one's eternal salvation is contained in this statement of the judicial sentence. And the reasoning of that sentence is exposed from those effects which argue to that cause, and provide witness to it. From these considerations we see, then, the reasoning for that sentence in Matthew 25 could not have been sought directly from the proper causes—such as God's decree, our calling, and our justification—without committing a clear ταυτολογία. Truly it would be nothing other than a tautology to say, "You who are called, and justified, and already destined for the kingdom of your Father, enter in now to your possession, because you have been called, because you have been justified, because you have been destined to the same."

There are not lacking most just reasons that God would deliver his judicial sentence according to our works. For our works are more observable, in as much as they are effects, than are the actual causes for that sentence. Indeed, God wants everything in that judgment to be visible and knowable by experience. Moreover, all men are hypocrites by nature, and so are tempted to present to others a hollow appearance of faith. This is why James says: "Show me your faith by your works" (Jas. 2:18). And finally, provided we understand in this life that God's future judgment in the next is according to works, we are deterred from evil deeds and stirred up to the pursuit of good works. From these considerations it should be clear that the sentence of life in the last judgment will be according to works not as causes of that life, but as most noteworthy effects of those proper causes—for example, the foreknowledge of God, predestination, calling, and justification—to be manifested to the whole world.

Now if it is asked whether that sentence to be delivered on the last day is one of life only, or whether it is one of justice as well, I respond: It is apparent from Scripture that the sentence which will be made at that time is chiefly one of life. "Come," Scripture says, "you who are blessed of my Father, and inherit the kingdom which has been prepared for you." In justification, admittedly, there is a sentence made of both justice and of life as a result of that justice. The sentence of justice is summed up in this present life—according to it we are already fully justified, if you consider justice by itself. The sentence of life [which belongs to justification], on the other hand, likewise, in truth, begins to be produced and delivered in this life. But because the sentence of eternal life does not achieve full execution in this life, that sentence must be especially repeated, and simultaneously fulfilled, on that final Day of Judgment. Yet I do not deny entirely that a verdict of righteousness too will be brought forward on that Day of Judgment, since we see in Matthew 12:32 that forgiveness of sins might be refused in the age to come. But it will be brought forward according to works inasmuch as such works are effects that will make known that true and solitary meritorious cause, Christ with his own righteousness apprehended by faith—or according to works as such are proofs of justification itself through faith, proofs, that is, that we have already in this life been justified by faith. There will, then, be no other sentence of justification which is according to future works than that which is a certain declaration of justification properly so called, which justification has already occurred and been perfected in this life.

Indeed, the word justification is received in two ways, properly and improperly. The term is used properly when we say that we are justified with reference to the cause of such, and thus the term is used by Paul throughout Romans. The term is used improperly when we say that we are justified with reference to the effects of such. And this is nothing other than to make it known that we have already through faith and the genuine cause of justification been justified, and this is necessarily declared by what is produced from justification. And thus the term justification is received in James 2:21. "Was not," James says, "Abraham justified according to works, when he offered his son Isaac upon the altar?" That is, was he not shown to be already justified through faith in Christ, and this from what was produced by justification (which is through faith), when he offered his son Isaac upon the altar. And that James in this text understands the word justification as the declaration of gratuitous justification in Christ appears from the same chapter, vs. 18, when he says: "Show me your faith by your works." Behold! Works demonstrate and declare faith, and through faith is justification, but works do not properly justify. Thus, to conclude, we do not deny that a certain verdict also of righteousness, or rather a declaratory verdict of that sentence of righteousness through faith which has already been given in this life, will be pronounced on that final Day of Judgment. But we say that Scripture particularly directs our attention to that sentence of life [rather than righteousness] which will be delivered at that future time. And thus we prefer, while not receding from a Scriptural phrase, to say with Scripture that a sentence of life will be pronounced on that future day of judgment. Thus far concerning good works.

Bibliography

PRIMARY SOURCES

Augustine. "On Marriage and Concupiscence." In *Saint Augustin: Anti-Pelagian Writings*, edited by Philip Schaff et al., 257–308. A Select Library of the Nicene and Post-Nicene Fathers of the Early Church (Series 1) 5. Peabody, MA: Hendrickson, 1994.

Braun, Johannes. *Doctrina foederum, sive Systema theologiae didacticae & elencticae; perspicua atque facili methodo*. Amsterdam: Henricum Wetstenium, 1702.

Burgess, Anthony. *The doctrine of original sin asserted & vindicated against the old and new adversaries thereof*. London: Abraham Miller, 1658.

Howie, Robert. *De reconciliatione hominis cum Deo*. Basel: Sebastian Henric Petri, 1591.

Medina, Bartolomé de. *Expositio in primam secundae angelici doctoris D. Thomae Aquinatis*. Salamanca, 1582.

Perkins, William. *Armilla aurea: id est, theologiae descriptio mirandam feriem causarum & salutis & damnationis iuxta verbum Dei proponens*. Cambridge: John Legate, 1590.

———. *Armilla aurea: id est, theologiae descriptio mirandam feriem causarum & salutis & damnationis iuxta verbum Dei proponens*. 2nd ed. Cambridge: John Legate, 1591.

Polanus, Amandus. *Partitiones theologicae juxta naturalis methodi Leges conformatae duobus libris, quorum primus est de Fide: alter de bonis Operibus*. Basil: Conrad Waldkirch, 1590.

Rollock, Robert. *Analysis dialectica Roberti Rolloci Scoti, ministri Iesu Christi in Ecclesia Edinburgensi, in Pauli Apostoli Epistolam ad Romanos*. Edinburgh: Robert Waldegrave, 1593.

———. *Analysis logica in epistolam Pauli apostoli ad Galatas*. London: Felix Kyngstonus, 1602.

Bibliography

———. *Analysis logica in epistolam ad Hebraeos.* Edinburgh: Henry Charteris, 1605.
———. *Commentarius . . . in epistolam Pauli ad Collossenses.* Edinburgh: Robert Waldegrave, 1600.
———. *An exposition upon some select Psalmes of David.* Edinburgh: Robert Waldegrave, 1600.
———. *In epistolam Pauli apostoli ad Ephesios . . . commentarius.* Edinburgh: Robert Waldegrave, 1590.
———. *In epistol[as] . . . ad Thessalonicenses priorem [et ad Thessalonicenses posteriorem, et ad Philemonem]commentarius.* Edinburgh: Robert Waldegrave, 1598.
———. *In evangelium Domini nostri Iesu Christi secundum Sanctum Iohannem.* Geneva: Le Preux, 1599.
———. *In librum Danielis prophetae . . . commentarius* Edinburgh: Robert Waldegrave, 1591.
———. *In selectos aliquot Psalmos Davidis . . . commentarius.* Geneva: Le Preux, 1599.
———. *Lectures upon the first and second Epistles of Paul to the Thessalonians.* Edinburgh: Robert Charteris, 1606.
———. *Select Works of Robert Rollock.* Edited by William M. Gunn. 2 vols. Grand Rapids, MI: Reformation Heritage, 2008.
———. *Tractatus de vocatione efficaci.* Edinburgh: Robert Waldegrave, 1597.
———. *A treatise of Gods effectual calling.* London: Felix Kyngstonus, 1603.
———. *Quaestiones et responsiones aliquot de Foedere Dei, deque Sacramento quod foederis Dei sigillum est.* Edinburgh: Henry Charteris, 1596.
Turretin, Francis. *Institutes of Elenctic Theology*, vol. 1. Translated by George Giger. Edited by James Dennison Jr. Phillipsburg, NJ: P & R, 1992.

SECONDARY LITERATURE

Backus, Irena. "Piscator Misconstrued: Some Remarks on Robert Rollock's 'Logical Analysis' of Hebrews 9." *Journal of Medieval and Renaissance Studies* 14, no. 1 (1984) 113–19.
Baker, J. Wayne. *Heinrich Bullinger and the Covenant.* Athens, OH: Ohio University Press, 1980.
Bell, M. Charles. *Calvin and Scottish Theology: The Doctrine of Assurance.* Edinburgh: Handsel, 1985.
Denlinger, Aaron Clay. "Calvin's Understanding of Adam's Relationship to His Posterity: Recent Affirmations of the Reformer's 'Federalism' Evaluated." *Calvin Theological Journal* 44 (2009) 226–50.
———. *Omnes in Adam ex pacto Dei: Ambrogio Catarino's Doctrine of Covenantal Solidarity and Its Influence on Post-Reformation Reformed Theologians.* Göttingen: Vandenhoeck & Ruprecht, 2010.

Bibliography

———. "Robert Rollock on Covenant and Sacrament: Two Texts." *Reformation & Renaissance Review* 15, no. 2 (2013) 199–211.

———. "Robert Rollock's Catechism on God's Covenant." *Mid-America Journal of Theology* 20 (2009) 105–29.

Ellis, Brannon. "The Eternal Decree in the Incarnate Son: Robert Rollock on the Relationship between Christ and Election." In *Reformed Orthodoxy in Scotland: Essays on Scottish Theology 1560–1775*, edited by Aaron Clay Denlinger, 45–65. London: Bloomsbury T. & T. Clark, 2015.

Fesko, J. V. *The Theology of the Westminster Assembly: Historical Context and Theological Insights*. Wheaton, IL: Crossway, 2014.

———. *Beyond Calvin: Union with Christ and Justification in Early Modern Reformed Theology (1517–1700)*. Göttingen: Vandenhoeck & Ruprecht, 2012.

Garner, Mark. "Preaching as a Communicative Event: A Discourse Analysis of Sermons by Robert Rollock (1555–1599)." *Reformation & Renaissance Review* 9, no. 1 (2007) 45–70.

Horton, Michael. "Law, Gospel, and Covenant: Reassessing Some Emerging Antitheses." *Westminster Theological Journal* 64 (2002) 279–87.

Isbell, R. Sherman. "The Origin of the Concept of the Covenant of Works." MA thesis, Westminster Theological Seminary, 1976.

Letham, Robert. "The *Foedus Operum*: Some Factors Accounting for Its Development." *Sixteenth Century Journal* 14, no. 4 (1983) 457–67.

Macedo, Breno Lucena. "The Covenant Theology of Robert Rollock." ThM thesis, Puritan Reformed Theological Seminary, 2012.

McGiffert, Michael. "The Perkinsian Moment of Federal Theology." *Calvin Theological Journal* 29, no. 1 (1994) 117–48.

Miller, Perry. *Errand into the Wilderness*. Cambridge, MA: Harvard University Press, 1956.

Muller, Richard. "The Covenant of Works and the Stability of Divine Law in Seventeenth-Century Reformed Orthodoxy: A Study in the Theology of Herman Witsius and Wilhelmus a Brakel." *Calvin Theological Journal* 29 (1994) 75–101.

Rolston, Holmes, III. "Responsible Man in Reformed Theology: Calvin versus the Westminster Confession." *Scottish Journal of Theology* 23 (1970) 129–56.

Woolsey, Andrew. "Robert Rollock (1555–1598): Principal, Theologian, and Preacher." In *Select Works of Robert Rollock*, vol. 1, edited by William M. Gunn, 1–24. Grand Rapids, MI: Reformation Heritage, 2008.

———. *Unity and Continuity in Covenantal Thought: A Study in the Reformed Tradition to the Westminster Assembly*. Grand Rapids, MI: Reformation Heritage, 2012.

www.ingramcontent.com/pod-product-compliance
Lightning Source LLC
Chambersburg PA
CBHW070935160426
43193CB00011B/1693